Insights

by Herbert Windolf

Through Kindle Direct Publishing:
Thoughts
Searching
Shadows and Light
Insights

Private Printing:
Biography – Bridges Across Times and Continents

Published by Verlag für Tiefenpsychologie und Anthropologie:
Brücken über Zeiten und Kontinente,
Biography – with Dorothea Rutkowsky

Planetary Studies Foundation Quarterly
Travelogues:
A Hike in Provence
A Safari Through Namibia
Alaska, the Last Terrestrial Frontier of the US
Galápagos
Excursions in Saxony's Switzerland
Monumental Sights, in Grand Staircase/Escalante, Utah, and Northernmost Arizona
Journey to Sumatra
Zambezi
Moroccan Impressions
The Lure of Africa
Tanzania Redux, unpublished

Planetary Studies Foundation Quarterly
Ten Explorations, six published:
The likely Futility of S.E.T.I. Programs
Snowball Earth
Wondrous Water
The Probability for Intelligent Life in the Universe
A Personal View of Existentialism
Tsunami
Pragmatism
Forty billion Potentially Habitable Planets
Exceptionalism
December 26, 1776

Annemarie Schnitt - Willkommen Website
Translations of Poems and Stories

Unpublished – for Private Use
Autobiography
Translations:
The Texas War of Independence in 1836
by Herman Ehrenberg
Five Years Behind Barbed Wire
by Walter Hartmann
Letters to David Walter
Heinrich Himmler, by Franz Wegener
Ukraine Letters, by Hans Windolf
Germany's Final Months of WWII, Diary of Hans Windolf
The Forgotten Generation, by Sabine Bode
War's Grandchildren, by Sabine Bode
Genesis, by Dorothea Rutkowsky

Courses facilitated:
From the Spice Trade to Globalization
Cataclysms and Extinctions
The Likely Futility of SETI Programs
The Cambrian Explosion
Human Evolution and Migration
The American National Mind vis-à-vis the Rest of the World

Addendum
in Thoughts
A Collection of Haiku Verses

Addendum
in Searching
Three African Stories

Addendum
in Shadows and Light
Ten Explorations

Content:

Introduction

Part I

Poetic Prose and Poetry

Table of Contents

Table of Contents Page:

Table of Contents   **Page:**

Table of Contents   **Page:**

Table of Contents

Table of Contents

Part II

Comments

Part III

Autobiography
Introduction

Part I: I have given this ninth volume of my Poetic Prose, or Prosetrie, as I call it tongue-in-cheek, the title *Insights*. In more than 1,700 verses I have explored and revealed my mind in memories, desires, concerns, missed opportunities, failures, accomplishments, what I strive, or have striven for, and what not. My psychology sister-in-law, Dorothea Rutkowsky, in Berlin, has called the venture psycho-hygienics, an apt name. As I have expressed several times in my verses, I write, foremost for myself. Another indication of my awareness.

Some of my writings are, what I would call, idle or humorous thoughts. But whenever possible I have tried to slip in a meaningful twist, as I sometimes have slyly done in many other verses. The majority of verses, however, do represent my inner workings. To publicize those, to reveal who I am, require guts, require a self-assurance I did not have in the past. At eighty-four years of age little matters anymore. Whoever reads these words, let him or her think whatever they wish. I am who I am!

Part II of this book lists twelve Comments, as I call them, elicited from some of my reader-friends. Some were volunteered, which gave me the audacious idea to ask for more. My intention was to find out whether and how I struck a chord with my writings, how my readers felt, what is, in a different context, expressed in a message from Maria Shriver I take permission to quote it here:

"I want to know what moves you, what you are looking forward to, what brings you delight, what tugs at your heart strings, what gets you up in the morning.

I want to know about both your dreams and your fears." . . . as they relate to my poems! I want to touch you. If not physically, then your mind.

While I received various kudos, nice as they are, I regretted the paucity of "revelations" which arrived in the Comments. I still wonder: How come?

In **Part III** find my autobiography written in 2004/2005 in the course of three months. Amended here and there, entries petered out by 2007, to be replaced by my poetic writings serving as autobiographical extensions.

Quite a few of my verses deal with death. Some of my friends urge me to let this subject be. "Every day is a new day", as one said. But if one has dealt with more than twenty-five afflictions, small and large, through the past fifteen years, with new health problems showing up through the weeks and months, it is a *Matter of Fact*, as I write in one poem. In another, the *Slow Lane*, I write of slow death versus a heart attack or stroke. I am comfortable writing about death. My life, while not complete, has been full. I have few regrets, except for the pain and sorrow I have caused others.

Thus, when I have named this book *Insights*, it is not that it is full of wisdom, no, just full of more of my babble. May you, my odd reader, not grow tired of it. The time will come when I will write no more.

Herbert Windolf   Prescott, AZ

July 1953

Epiphany

At seventeen I was in Sweden,
stood on a jetty, facing west.
The sun was setting, wind was blowing,
the sea was rough – I was at rest!
I stood there for the longest time
and sang into the wind.
Then, more and more, something did happen,
wide open did become my mind.
So wide that it included all,
while I was every part of it.
I was the world, the world was I,
this, what my spirit now beheld.
A feeling was it – wonderful –
too difficult for me to tell.

How did it happen, came to being?
Much later did I understand.
It was the setting and my singing,
which so enchanted and entranced
and took me to this far-off land!

"Yeah, my soul went free, and, wheeling like an eagle,
I saw indeed that there was no Teshoo Lama,
nor any other soul.
As a drop draws to water, so my soul drew near
to the Great Soul which is beyond all Hind,
from Ceylon in the sea to the Hills,
and my own painted rock at Such-zen;
I saw evert camp and village, to the least,
were we have ever rested.
I saw them at one time and in one place;
for they were within the soul.
By this I knew the soul had passed beyond
the illusion of time and space and of things.
By this I knew that I was free."
Rudyard Kipling, Kim

Infinity 1

I sit on a boulder in my yard,
Rikki behind me exploring her world.
Conscious awareness is mine while it lasts.
The wind sings to me in the bushes and trees,
a bouquet of yellow flowers grows next to my feet.
All this must end, no more sensations,
no longer being of this world, no more observations.
Yet I can't help imagining what all I have been,
what my molecules, my elements have already seen.
Did some trod the Earth in a triceratops,
and before grace a carboniferous fern?
What will yet happen to my few remains?
The biome of my very Self
will, too, go the way of all earthly things,
expire in the flames the fire will bring.

But then,
somewhere away from the rush of the world,
my ashes will be dispersed by the wind,
rain will wash some into the earth.
Will my molecules, my atoms, my elements,
nourish yet other beings in life's marvelous sea,
a nematode in the soil, a leaf on a tree?
Will a browsing doe's milk feed her fawn yet to be?
Might I grace the world in a flower's bloom?
Lucky me if a tree's roots take me in
and in a juniper I live for a few hundred years.
I shall be recycled, it's nature's design,
in the Earth, in Life, engulfed by the sun.
I am infinite.
Infinity is mine.

At the touch of love everyone becomes a poet.
Plato

Loki,

I've been called by my psycho-friend Norm.
The god of Norse mythology.
A trickster he was
making trouble for the Asgard gods.
He could change shape,
even sex, as he pleased.
Well, I change the meaning,
the shape of my words,
but sex I rather leave alone.
To make my point,
don't believe all that I say,
since I twist and turn, the words I play.
But come the day,
know what to pick of what I say.
And as far as similarity goes,
I must remember Loki's woes
when he had to face his final throes.

During times of universal deceit,
telling the truth becomes a revolutionary act.
George Orwell

Jesters

In various cultures a character appears
who has the license or takes it as he pleases,
to challenge, provoke, and to tease,
his fellow-contemporaries, even authorities.
There is Loki, the minor Asgard god,
who troubled his fellow deities to no good.
The court jester of medieval times
was allowed to speak his mind,
within limits, of course,
to the king and princes at their gatherings,
frequently uncivil and raucous.
The Yiddish Bodkin in eastern Jewish villages
in general and at celebrating events,
treated his fellows and friends
to insults, often coarse.
They had to take them.
There was no remorse.

In life, it's important to know when to stop arguing
with people and simply let them be wrong.
Unknown

Fiction

My editor friends keep urging me
to try my hand at writing fiction.
I have translated fiction, biographies, and poetry,
written my autobiography and a biography,
science articles and travelogues.
Whatever I have written deals with reality.
Most, but not all, of my so-called poetry, does,
except for a few escapes into the wilds of imagination.
Not being true poetry,
I have come to call it poetic prose,
using meter and rhyme.
My attempts at writing fiction,
in my opinion, turned out too dry.
I'm just too factual a guy.

More gold has been mined from the minds of men
than has been taken from the Earth.
Napoleon Hill

Number Nine

Here we are. Number eight of my books
of about fifteen hundred poetic prose
is almost finished, ready to go.
Will I have time to finish one more collection,
come up with enough ideas, have sufficient mojo?
Will my ever new ailments keep me ambling along,
telling the not-so-rim-greaper's knocking wrong?

You should always say much more than you mean,
and always mean much more than you say.
Oscar Wilde

Capriccio Italien

Sitting on my couch in the morning
was floating up in my brain,
a long forgotten piece of music
I many times listened to in my teenage days.
Calling up Tchaikovsky, I found my lead,
understood the composition's call to my mood,
being returned to times gone by.
What I interpreted, perceived,
was a longing, a promise, a struggle,
a becoming, and fulfillment.
And this is what I did!
I also realized that I had discovered classical music
before my early twenties in Beethoven and Bach.

The Capriccio Italien is free in form,
lively, fast and intense.
It must have conveyed to me
in these early years
that which I found as years went by.

A man is not old as long as he is seeking something.
Jean Rostand

Motto

The new motto for the U.S.A.,
will no longer be "E pluribus unum,"
"From many one,"
but rather the more called for:
"Semper paratus,"
"Always ready,"
if ever this will come.

Sometimes people carry to such perfection
the mask they have assumed that in due course
they actually become the person they seem.
William Somerset Maugham

Bugs

No, not Bugs Bunny of cartoon fame,
but anything from viruses to bacteria and insects,
we colloquially call these days by this name.
With Covid-19 now a rampant brew,
when I call my friends I ask:
"Are you still bug-free,
or need I call the exterminator for you"?

The first condition for immortality is death.
Stanislaw Jerzy Lec

Wicked

Help me, help me, I can't do without.
Humorous associations keep popping up.
Most times they leave a laugh behind.
At others they put me into a bind.
It's just that I have a wicked mind.

When choosing between two evils
I always like to take the one
I've never tried before.
Mae West

Loan

I lent my son four thousand dollars
to buy himself a car.
He's good for it, I'm certain,
and paid back two thousand, so far.
But I claim just for the fun of it
that I still own half of this car.
I'm just not sure whether its the front or back,
the left or the right of his "jaguar."

The little I know I owe to my ignorance.
Sacha Guitry

Modus Vivendi

We have found a modus vivendi,
a way to make do.
Or better, an arrangement to peacefully coexist
until, maybe,
a better way we may come to see.
Hope springs eternally.

We never love heartily but once,
and that is the first time we love.
Jean de La Bruyere

The Way

Plenty of ways can be found in plain sight,
others, like ubiquitous, are tucked away.
Not everything is going my way,
other ways simply lead you astray.
To find one's way important it is,
if no way found out, may end in misery.
There is the parting of ways,
being born that way.
Sinatra's I did it My Way.
A one-way street's direction
we must obey.
You won't believe how many ways there are,
with the Milky Way being full of stars.
And to conclude this exposé,
there's Bacharach's and Warwick's
Way to San Jose.

That man is richest whose pleasures are cheapest.
Henry David Thoreau

Evil and Good

I've turned it around
how it's usually understood.
So, what are we humans mostly?
Evil or good?
Destruction is evil
its gratification instant,
its results lethal.
Having the choice between good and evil,
the choice for excitement, immediate fun,
for that's what it is,
takes many to this hit-and-run.
Building takes time,
its gratification is sublime.
Is this the reason for evil to chime?
That building and caring
require thought and patience.
A very different paradigm.

Even the voice of conscience undergoes mutation.
Stanislaw Jerzy Lec

Me

If you want to know who I am,
where I'm coming from,
read my poetic prose
of fourteen hundred verses and some.
If you can stand the mix,
often serious, sometimes fun,
for I love an intriguing pun.
But it's the serious ones that count,
their meaning, their thoughts are paramount.
I write for myself first, as I've said before,
to retrieve from my mind
that which waits to be born.
I have learned a bundle writing this stuff.
I'm glad we have Google
to separate truth, as far as it goes,
from today's all too present chaff.

All great truths begin as blasphemies.
George Bernard Shaw

Nerves

Afternoons or evenings,
with friends together
in a lively conversation,
it's fun to partake,
but then leaves me at nighttime
wide awake.
Easily riled up, I go awry.
I'm just too sensitive a guy.

The difference between stupidity and genius is
that genius has its limits.
Albert Einstein

Ideology, Idols and Idolatry

Meanings change.
Ideology, once understood
as a set of beliefs, of philosophies,
is today viewed critically, condemnatory.
The reason is its trending, its proximity to an idol,
an object of extreme devotion,
of worship, a false god or conception, a fallacy.
From there it is one more step to idolatry,
the worship of a physical object as a god,
an immoderate attachment or devotion.

To accomplish great things, you must not only act,
but also dream,
not only dream but also believe.
Anatole France

Freedom

The right to think, speak, and act
as one desires without hindrance.
The ideal of freedom in the U.S.A.
has been degraded,
has become an idol, an idolatry.
It is worshipped,
has become disengaged from reality,
the rational application of its right.
It has become a "Thing in itself."

The problem with the world is that fools and fanatics
are always so certain of themselves,
and wiser people so full of doubts.
Bertrand Russell

Occipital Bun

It has been found that Neandertals had one.
A bump on the back of their skull.
A few years ago it was found that
people of European extraction
have inherited up to three percent
of Neandertal DNA.
This is an indication that between
Homo Neanderthalensis and Home sapiens
some hanky-panky went on.
Well, I should have known this all along
for I do have a little occipital bun.

Man – a creature made at the end of the week's work
when God was tired.
Mark Twain

Shadows

Once more sitting on my rock,
I see shadows flitting over the ground.
I need not look up
for I know what they are about.
A flock of bushtits are making their rounds.

The best part of beauty
is that which no picture can express.
Francis Bacon

Science Fiction

I've read SF, as it is called, since my early teens.
It helped me broaden my mind.
Some folks have expressed disdain for it,
it shows in what they left behind.
I went for the science in SF.
Space opera and fantasy
never attracted me.

The false is nothing
but an imitation of the true.
Marcus Tulles Cicero

Ninety

Now that my hemolytic anemia
and Meniere's disease is stable, under control,
and provided my heart does not go A.W.O.L,
I may have a few more years
to live, as a goal
than I thought possible a couple of years ago.
That's why I decided to bite the sour apple
and follow the orthopedic surgeon's advice
to have my left knee replaced,
never mind the temporary sacrifice.
I'm shooting now for ninety,
will be rolling the dice,
and hope that I'm not living in a fool's paradise.

It is a capital mistake to theorize before one has data.
Insensibly one begins to twist facts to suit theories,
instead of theories to suit facts.
Arthur Conan Doyle

Ode to Birds

I love and admire all these birds,
most in nature I observed.
There is the gannet with its diving panache
the brown pelican for its headlong dash
the loon with its haunting voice
ravens cavorting in the sky
smart crows with their raucous cries
the puffins, painted clowns of the seas
mourning doves pursuing mates
the eagle for its soaring might
humming birds in their fancy flight
the bushtits flitting through the trees
minor goldfinches going for thistle seed
owls hooting in the early morn
phainopeplas catching insects in the sky
a Cooper hawk dashing for its prey
the road runner for its funny gait
the turkey vulture for its circling flight
the blue jay chasing other birds away
house finches in their plenitude

the grosbeaks for their plump demeanor
towhees in their seed pursuit
lazuli buntings passing through
penguins flying through the water
blue-footed boobies in their mating dance
grebes of their walking-on-water prance
the albatross on its epic journeys
ostriches running across the veldt
bee eaters in their loamy burrows
a red-wing blackbird, companion for a few days
a meadow lark singing her life away in the sky
queleas flocking in the thousands
cranes stalking their prey in the shallows
the secretary bird hunting in the grass
gulls, always hungry, everywhere
lilac-breasted rollers in their fancy dress
king fishers catching a fish in a dash
weaver birds in their copious nests
kori bustards, with their funny name
storks building their high-up nests
parrots, gorgeous in flight and at rest
nightingales singing sweetly at dusk

ducks in their many kinds
storks rattling along the Rhine
oxpeckers pecking for insects and blood
flickers hammering on the boards of the house
robins bobbing in their search for worms
titmice coming for a grain at a time
the peregrine falcon in its headlong dive
cranes flying straight-necked in the sky
geese for V-formation try
starlings in fantastic murmurations
frigates, thieving in the skies
the dipper diving for tidbits in a stream
quails with their wailing call
a kookaburra alighting on a rail
the wren twittering here and there
condors soaring high in the air
cormorants diving for their food
cardinals, bright red in their suit
cassowaries to avoid
cuckoos calling in Tuscan woods
pigeons out for their daily food
a waxwing flock raiding my pyracantha bush

guinea hens flocking through the brush
nuthatches climbing trees
the plenitude of birds-of-paradise
Galapagos finches in their variety.
All this evolution has wrought
from dinosaurs to today's multitude.

They do not love that do not show their love.
Marcel Achard

Mesoamerican Cultures

The Aztecs were the worst of the lot,
ripping beating hearts from the living body
dripping of blood,
all to appease their imagined god.
No matter their achievements –
to thus sacrifice people wholesale is absurd!
I don't care for their pompous architecture
lacking aesthetics.
And why does man need to build hight into the sky
from time immemorial to the present day?
Their mathematics, agriculture and hydraulic engineering
are admirable but don't make up for their other failings.
Having studied anthropology
I could never bring myself to become interested
in these Indian cultures, had no want.
I do not pine for them
having been wiped from the Earth.
It is good they are gone.

Those who can make you believe absurdities
can make you commit atrocities.
Voltaire

Say Something

These days, heading for eighty-four,
I often think or express out loud:
"Say something,"
with my processing ability, my patience or willingness
to listen to an ongoing discourse or lengthy article
running out.
More and more I use Fast Forward,
or read only the last paragraph of an article,
enough to know what it is about.
This, too, may be a reason why writing fiction
never made my day.
As I've said "I'm just too factual a guy."
My thinking is reflected in my Poetic Prose.
Rarely do I manage to write a poetic poem.
Reality is my forté.
In poetic prose I can express, usually briefly,
an insight, an idea,
it being my very me.

The accent of a man's native country remains in his mind and his
heart,
as it does in his speech.
Francois de La Rochefoucauld

Digger

There is this nice neighbor of mine, Bob, by name,
who is whacking at his bushes a lot.
He likes best, haha, mountain mahogany
which he tirelessly digs out underground.
I told him, "Bob, the way you go
pretty soon I will look all the way
into your bathroom, hoho."
To honor him, I call him my Whacko.

Tact in audacity consists in knowing how far we may go too far.
Jean Cocteau

Incoherence

It appears that U.S. American society
is split into four social groups:
the Christian-based assemblage,
the economic complex, the scientific community,
and the broad, fluid swath of non-affiliated individuals.
The interests of the four groups are not
internally unified, at times overlap,
at other times diverge, sometimes violently.
This frequent lack of coherence,
the shortage of communal thinking
appears to manifest itself in ideologies
resulting in strife.

The average man does not know what to do with this life,
yet wants another one which will last forever.
Anatole France

Pathological Collective Identity

It seems that in the U.S.A.,
like in no other country of the world, ideas,
formulated thoughts or opinions, become ideologized.
There's birth control, gun possession, global warming,
and now the wearing of covid masks.
Identity is expressed by what makes
a group or person different from others.
Ideology is a set of beliefs
upon which an organizational system is based.
Three of the above ideas are vigorously rejected
by conservative organizations.
Religious orientation appears to be at the root of rejection,
supplemented by economic preferences.
Collective identity confers a sense of belonging
to its adherents.

Strong collective identity produces
a lack of individual identity,
a "making up of one's mind" about things.
The conformity of thought
becomes pathological collective identity.
It is a manifestation of insecurity.
Insecurity is an expression of fear.

Change alone is eternal, perpetual, immortal.
Arthur Schopenhauer

Pathological Individualism

Individualism prioritizes personal goals
as opposed to those of a society.
It proposes the right of the individual
to freedom and self-realization.
It is an ideology.
When individualism is carried to the extreme
it becomes destructive and pathological,
detrimental to the rational functioning of society.

Let us enrich ourselves with our mutual differences.
Paul Valery

Anticipating

I've followed a motto for most of my life,
to think ahead to what may arrive.
Nothing's assured the way we expect,
and it may not suffice to merely react.
That's why I didn't operate blind,
rather followed my motto below:
"If I'm not ahead, I will be behind."

They say that in the end truth will triumph, but it's a lie.
Anton Chekov

Handshake

The Covid pandemic put a stop to shake hands.
When all is over, said, and done,
I hope the handshake will also be gone.
I've always wondered where the other hand had been
before offered to me in a gesture of esteem.
The Japanese have got it right
facing each other at a short distance,
and with a slight bow express respect, are polite.
I hope Covid-19 will see the handshake's twilight
being replaced by a more pleasant rite.

All is in the hands of man.
Therefore wash them often.
Stanislaw Jerzy Lec

Keystone Species

As a keystone prevents an arch from collapse,
so do keystone species
keep their respective environments intact.
Often they are predatory, at the food chain's top,
like the sea otter in the kelp forest,
keeping sea urchins in check.
Bears dragging nourishing salmon carcasses
into the Pacific Northwest forests,
and starfish controlling the near-seashore.
Wolves in Yellowstone Park,
and bass in freshwater streams.
But herbivores can act the same,
as wildebeest do in the Serengeti.
Remove them, and their environment
becomes impoverished, does even collapse.
Another creature at the very top of the food chain,
oft not-so-sapient Man,
the most predatory, if you don't mind,
is on an opposite trajectory.

Increasing its numbers manifold
it goes against nature's keystone rule,
by diminishing the food chain's base,
replacing creatures large and small,
with cattle, pigs and chickens,
wheat, rice, and maize, monocultures all.

If you create an act, you create a habit.
If you create a habit, you create a character.
If you create a character, you create destiny.
William Makepeace Thackery

Traits

Also called habits, even addictions, at times.
Some are pleasant, some benign,
some are obsessive, others destructive,
some are a nuisance to the world around,
and some are a detriment to the one thus spellbound.
An affliction it is which may need to be told.
It calls for its weighing of right or wrong.
If right, for insight and awareness,
then acceptance along.
Yet with all the afore not all is done.
What is then required is Will, sufficiently strong,
to whenever the trait manifests itself,
to promote the awareness to check the Wrong.
Will is what it takes to change that which ails.

To escape criticism do nothing, say nothing, be nothing.
Elbert Hubbard

Open Door

In my formative years, my teens,
I grew up in a household,
my grandmother's grocery store,
a place open to the world.
Neighbors drifted in for a purchase, a chat,
friends and relatives showed up on the spot.
The door always open,
I was conditioned by that.
It followed me into my later years.
When a neighbor shows up,
a friend, or person I know,
or someone with a matter I care to pursue,
I open my door and invite them in. -
There are people I know
who conduct whatever business
only through a gap of their door.
Conditioned they are by wherever they dwelled.
Trust has failed them
and their openness to the world.
What do the recesses of their minds behold?

Our memories are independent of our wills.
Richard Brinsley Sheridan

Idiosyncratic

Rikki, my companion for more than three years,
born after Christmas of two-thousand-fifteen,
was adopted and returned to the Society
likely because the previous adopters
had bee unable to handle this feline.
Thus, I fell in love with her
when she was already a year old.
She's a Calico-Tortie cat,
with a soft, white chest patch,
white belly, four white paws,
symmetric as it goes.
She's the most idiosyncratic cat
of the eight I have had.
Another word describing her is "tortitude."

Do not be afraid of beasts, but friends —
as the beast will wound your body,
but a friend will wound your soul.
Buddha

Languid 1

Being laid-up by Covid-19,
for four months now unable to see
friends, up close, for a little spree.
There's only so much you are able to do
cooped up in the home, by email and phone,
and a decrepit knee keeps you down.
Thus a languidness, a fatigue, has crept in.
This isolation will likely go on.
A few more months
and I will be ready for the looney bin.

The madness of individuals is an exception.
The madness of groups, parties, nations and epochs
is a rule.
Friedrich Nietzsche

Abuse

Many a child grows up wronged and abused.
Lucky the ones who simply grow up
with or without support.
The wronged-ones
likely carry their pain throughout their lives.
Some never become aware of their hurt,
yet it smolders in their being,
while others work through it for a positive turn.
A few express it in anger and hate.
Some have the will to leave anger behind.
Others cultivate it, telling the world,
again and again, how they were wronged,
never to take responsibility
for what's troubling their mind.
Rather they keep heaping abuse on those
who cross their path, who may be kind.

The greatest weariness comes from work not done.
Eric Hoffer

Taking for Granted

Fail I did to appreciate well
what I once found in a struggle, a spell,
expressed by not needing a wedding ring.
It somehow lasted for decades on end.
Had I only been aware
that it was a gift, a grant.

People change and forget to tell each other.
Lillian Hellman

Stimulus

Life thrives on stimuli,
food, sex, the arousal of nerves,
an external agent which incites activity,
to goad, to instigate, to provoke, to motivate.
Not necessarily a positive trait.
Stimuli, humans in gatherings and babbling, crave,
in extremis expressed in a rave.
Evolution has not taught us yet
discipline during a pandemic
for that which we then cannot have.

Continuous effort – not strength or intelligence –
is the key to unlocking our potential.
Winston Churchill

Prosetry

---

is a word I created for my verses,
a combination of poetry and prose,
it's syllables connected in reverse.
With prose I use colloquial, factual language.
To express ideas and feelings it is poetry I choose.
Meter and rhyme are following close.
Thus, prosetry is a meeting of both.

Words are the small change of thought.
Jules Renard

Belonging, once more

This is the one poem representing me best,
I wrote about 20 years ago,
for myself, my own behest:

I am – born German
at home in America
yet at heart European
by intellect Western Man
human by species
member of all life by evolution
part of the universe by chemistry

I don't trust anyone who's nice to me
but rude to the waiter.
Because they would treat me the same way
if I were in that position.
Muhammad Ali

Infinity 2

I wrote of in Shadows and Light.
At the end of this poem I declaim:
"I am infinite.
Infinity is mine."
Eternal the elements of my body are,
many times reconstituted over time.
In a fleeting moment coming alive
in conscious awareness they fathom life.
To find truth, as far as it can be maintained,
what ephemeral life is all about,
versus all other storied claims.

Any fool can know.
The point is to understand.
Albert Einstein

Emory Oak

It must have been twenty-eight years ago
that I planted this tree in my yard.
Four feet tall being at the time,
it grew to at least twenty feet in height.
This year, precociously, an eight foot tall branch
grew straight up at its top.
I love to watch it reaching for the sky
swaying sensuously in the wind.
I wonder:
will it make it through the coming winter?
Will I see it growing stronger,
adding to its trunk,
to its beautiful build?

Youth is happy because it has the capacity to see beauty.
Anyone who keeps the ability to see beauty
never grows old.
Franz Kafka

Shapely

These days, at the ripe old age
of almost eighty-four,
I've noticed how much I like watching
the curves of shapely young maidens.
There isn't much sexual desire anymore,
it's rather the aesthetics I adore.
Yet there are some people
who think that's a sham
and rather call me a dirty old man.

A man is never more serious than when he praises himself.
Georg Christoph Lichtenberg

Anesthesia

Replacement surgery is coming up
for a knee no longer doing its job.
I must be put under
for the surgeon to cut.
Then I might wake up
with my mind off track.
Or I might be put to sleep
never to come back.
What a way to go
without regrets and without woe.

When you look long into an abyss,
the abyss looks into you.
Friedrich Nietzsche

Creatures of Habit

We are such creatures of habit,
I am no different by far.
But I think I am aware
of what most of my habits are.
I do change some as I please,
something in others I miss.
Some people are stuck to their habits,
oft funny to observe.
What it comes down to in the end,
is that they aren't aware,
live in a lala land.

Almost every man wastes part of his life
to display qualities he does not possess.
Samuel Johnson

Empathy

Remember the little spider
who spun his magnificent net
between cactus pots on my window sill?
And restored the web overnight,
when I thoughtlessly brushed it aside.
Well, never did he catch anything to eat.
The other day I had to straighten the cactus
from which he had bound his net,
in the process destroying the web.
Lo and behold, the following day,
there glittered in the light of the sun,
a new web the little spider had spun.
Smaller it was, out of oomph
he or she must have run,
not having caught food for life to go on.
The days before I had looked high and low,
to find an insect to feed the little fellow.
Alas, not one I could find.
Now I feel sorry for the little creature
I never got to see, who so valiantly tried and tried.

A friend is one before whom
I may think aloud.
Ralph Waldo Emerson

Navel Gazing

In sixteen-thirty, John Winthrop proclaimed
in Massachusetts Bay before his Puritans:
"We shall be a city upon a hill,
the eyes of all people are upon us."
Three hundred years later Ronald Reagan added
"shining" to the words,
implying that the United States
acted as a beacon of hope for the world.
Thus were the foundations of American
Exceptionalism laid.
Much good has come to the world from this idea,
but it came at the expense of a wider view,
its root cause
a self-indulgent, excessive purview.
The ideology claims that America
has a unique mission to transform the world.
Alas, American politicians are human, too,
and all too often failed to live up themselves
what they proclaimed to do.
Since Winthrop and Reagan the world has changed.
Other nations have risen, are better organized
and maintained.

The worst that arose from America's splendid idea
was, that the USA, all too often,
feels it can scoff at the world at large,
and thumbs its nose to the detriment of all.
Would it only be that this great nation
would realize that it is one of many,
and look beyond its borders north and south,
and the oceans east and west,
and quit navel gazing to its own best.

To believe you are magnificent.
And gradually to discover that you are not magnificent.
Enough labor for one human life.
Czeslaw Milosz

Perpetuum Mobile

It appears my writing will go on and on,
when I had thought that
after my first published volume I was done.
Friends teased me whenever I claimed
the current volume would be my last.
By now, I've decided
I shall write till the ink runs out
or whatever I am talking about.

Behind many acts that are thought ridiculous
there are wise and weighty motives.
François de La Rochefoucauld

Stories

When, oh when, are we going to learn,
to understand, to comprehend,
that we live by the stories
our fertile minds create?
Listen believers, whatever you think,
no deity gave it.
It came from no throne.
Nor is anything you believe
carved forever in stone.

Don't blame a clown for acting like a clown.
Blame yourself for going to the circus.
Unknown

Fortuna Imperatrix Mundi,

Carl Orff's opening of Carmina Burana,
freely translated to
"Fortuna, goddess of fortune, of luck,
Ruler of the World."
Bemoaned in the epic
as the inexorable fate ruling both gods and mortals.
In my younger years I was a firm believer
that what I accomplished was due to my doing.
At my current age of almost eighty-four,
it looks to me as if Fortuna
rules my life, more and more.
Is this the reason I enjoy listening
to the presentation of Carmina Burana,
its powerful score.

We the people are the rightful masters
of both Congress and the Courts,
not to overthrow the Constitution
but to overthrow the men who would
pervert the Constitution.
Abraham Lincoln

Social Lubricant

Most of what we do is babble.
A few hundred words suffice
to talk for the rabble.
A few thousand for an intelligent conversation is nice.
But we ought to be aware
that, for all I care,
at least eighty percent
is babble, the passing of inconsequential details,
a social lubricant..
Yet, it has made our societies ascent
ever so vast in extent.

Society has become so fake
that the truth actually bothers people.
Unknown

Wanted

What does it mean "To be wanted"?

Is it the desire "To be loved"?

It is more than a smidgen below the latter.

Is it then just acceptance we seek?

To belong,

to be wanted,

to be loved,

for our own sake?

When people appear to be something other
than good and decent, it is only because they are reacting
to stress, pain, or the deprivation of basic human needs
such as security, love, and self=esteem.
Abraham Maslow

Equanimity and Peace,

----

of mind, that is.
Mental calmness, composure,
and evenness of temper,
are goals for my remaining years.
One small activity, helped along by Covid-19,
very much appeals,
is to sit with RikkiCat at dusk,
on my front deck on one of my chairs,
or better for her,
at the bottom of my stairs.

In youth we run into difficulties.
In old age difficulties run into us.
Henry Wheeler Shaw

64

Lurking

You'll be surprised, if you so ken,
what lurks in the minds of women and men,
you, on first sight, considered sane.
How they coddle conspiracies, some arcane,
stories, beliefs, most to wash hogs,
at best in the derrière a pain.
Confronted by such bane, gloss it over.
Trying to change their minds they'll never deign.
Intelligent discourse will be in vein.

In life, it's important to know when to stop arguing
with people and simply let them be wrong.
Unknown

Zephyr,

---

zephyr, gentle wind.
Once the heat has abated
it caresses my skin.
How deprived would we be
without Zephyrus, Greek god,
on whose behest
we can enjoy
pleasant winds from the west.

Politicians showed wear sponsor jackets
like Nascar drivers,
then we know who owns them.
Robin Williams

Deities

Of the many deities invented by man
there were only fourteen in the Greek pantheon.
The Hindu make do with about thirty-four.
The Shinto get up to sixty-one.
There's creep in the north
with the Norse having sixty-four.
The Egyptians top it off
with one-thousand-five-hundred or more.
The Christians, when it comes down to it,
have truly three.
The Muslims, radicals that they are,
limit themselves to just Allah.
The numbers may vary here and there,
but the higher the number,
this is only fair.

I have noticed even people who claim
everything is predestined,
and that we can do nothing to change it,
look before they cross the road.
Stephen Hawking

Las Vegas

I've never been to Las Vegas,
the city of razzmatazz.
Were I given a trip there,
all free of charge,
I would gladly let it pass.
It's name translates to "The Meadows."
Personally, I, would rather walk meadows,
than cross he city of Las Vegas.

In America, they call it "lobbying."
Everywhere else in the world
they call it "bribery & corruption."
Unknown

Bloom

I have two tree-like Madagascar Palms,
with one, I guess, being forty years old.
The smaller one has gone into bloom.
Two clusters of large white blossoms erupted,
only three times in twenty-eight years.
At times. I catch a delicate scent,
unexpected from so large a plant.
The blossoms turn brown
and drop to the ground.
I wonder what kind of home
these two big trees will find when I am gone?
But more so, I hope,
I will see one more bloom
before I am gone.

Everyone gets so much information all day long
that they lose their common sense.
Gertrude Stein

Verbal Communication

---

is between a speaker and a listener.
When a speaker is droning on
interruption is warranted.
But if the listener interrupts the speaker
shortly after communication has commenced,
communication is likely no longer effective
with emotional issues triggered.
Once the listener interrupts,
he or she is no longer listening,
but is most likely projecting
his or her own thoughts
on the subject at issue.
To maintain reason is a difficult task.

Complaining about a problem without posing a solution
is called whining.
Teddy Roosevelt

"Nature,

----

red in tooth and claw."
So wrote Alfred Lord Tennyson
in eighteen-fifty.
Not only is Nature red in tooth and claw,
but it is raw,
in what it throws at us
in hurricanes, floods, pandemics, tsunamis,
volcanic eruptions, earthquakes, and more.
It is in our self-interest and it is our duty
to mitigate Nature's excesses,
without becoming excessive ourselves.
Yet, "raw," "throws," "mitigate," and "excesses"
are human value terms.
Nature simply "is."

When everything is coming your way,
you're in the wrong lane.
Steven Wright

71

Dirt

Those who pile dirt on an opponent's name
do it at the risk of soiling themselves
to their very own shame.
Instead of dumping dirt onto the other's floor,
they ought to sweep in front of their door.
What's worse is that they fail to see
the failure of their integrity.

When the debate is lost,
slander becomes the tool of the losers.
Socrates

Apparitions

There I lay in the hospital again,
my hemoglobin level moving about.
In my drug-induced daze I was no longer certain
whether it was day or night.
From time to time I opened my eyes
and thought apparitions, ghosts,
caretakers, were hovering over my bed,
then quickly fading, as if never having been there.
Was it all my subconscious desire
for care, for loving care?

We are more closely connected to the invisible
than the visible.
Novalis

Topsy-Turvy

The world's turned topsy-turvy,
what once was up's now down.
And after some halfway sane decades,
in came rushing the clowns.
The pandemic magnified the mess,
so that these days few places on Earth
truly know know how to address,
apply reason and sanity
to find forward looking ways
for better days
sorely required for humanity.

The human race has one really effective weapon,
and that is laughter.
Mark Twain

Lost

We take our health, our mobility, for granted,
most of us, so gifted, that is.
When it fails, when we find out the extent
to which we must rely on kind help,
only then do we realize
what we have lost.

Character is higher than intellect . . .
A great soul will be strong to live,
as well as to think.
Ralph Waldo Emerson

Roaming

I'm roaming existence.
What is it for? What is it about.
Why does life come into being?
What is evolution for?
Is there a hidden purpose?
None that I can perceive.
Maybe it's a terrible jest that
the universe's creator –
maybe long forgotten –
played on us poor semi-conscious creatures,
together with the gamut of life
the universe let come into being.
Just because all the elements for life were in abundance,
to play with, to make dinos come about,
and whatever else it grew over millions of years,
only – another play – to route.
It's been claimed that the universe –
simply material it is –
becomes conscious through us grubbing creatures
and whichever others there may be.

For thousands of years mankind
has probed what it thought there is, was, and may be,
the whys, the might-bes,
the where-froms, the how-sos, and other stories.
We think life's hunky dory, most of us do,
unless tragedy strikes,
and for a moment in time we lose our glory.
But, in truth, the universe is a violent place.
It doesn't give a damn whether a species,
a star, a galaxy, fails.
So, if this place of abode has no purpose at all,
is a joke when it comes down to it,
keeps its secrets hidden,
it is up to us to give our lives Purpose.
We must keep trying through glory and pain.

Even the voice of conscience undergoes mutation.
Stanislaw Jerzy Lec

Insights

An insight I cherish
of times long ago, was,
when in a conversation with my father
– his last visit in America –
we talked about a situation, a concern of his,
to which I eventually
– the conversation was brief –
responded that it was impossible for me
to penetrate, to sense, the feel,
that which he dealt with.
He agreed.
And to this day,
thirty-plus years ago,
I still heaven't forgotten this insight,
and am proud
– there are so few things to be proud of –
that, at this age, I had realized something,
something that took decades to grow.

God created man and, finding him not sufficiently alone,
gave him a companion to make him feel his solitude more
keenly.
Paul Valery

Short and Sweet

Brief but relevant it is so defined.
And I know my friend Nancy is similarly inclined.
Come to the point. Say what you've got to say,
don't bother me with straw and hay,
and what the two are turned into
once they've gone though a bovine's belly.

If you want to hide your face, walk naked.
Stanislaw Jerzy Lec
Stanislaw, i love your mottos.
H.W.

Alone

I feel alone.
A terrible punishment this is.
Was I really that amiss
to deserve this?
Some people, mostly women,
are happy in their solitude.
Men seem to need company
so as not to be struck by an often
not so temporary mood.

If you are lonely when you're alone,
you are in bad company.
Jean Paul Satre

Caring

There are two ways of caring.
An active one
which can easily become too much.
Do this, do that,
no, you are not in touch.
Then there is the passive one,
which lets the patient ask
for what she would like to have done, to see.
It is oft the better one
to let things simply be.

It is a capital mistake to theorize before one has data.
Insensibly one begins to twist facts to suit theories,
instead of theories to facts.
Arthur Conan Doyle

81

Waste

Our civilization will fall to its knees,
or lower, still, flat down,
if it does not curb the waste it produces,
in which we all will drown.
It cannot go on
the way we package and discard.
I'm glad when I'll be gone,
not seeing this beautiful globe
becoming an ugly junkyard.

God in his wisdom made the fly
and then forgot to tell us why.
Ogden Nash

Building vs Wrecking

Building something takes time.
The pleasure of experiencing something growing
can be sublime.
Wrecking something, oft so quick,
brings instantaneous satisfaction.
Is this why individuals and societies
in their pursuit of destruction
appear to some of us, at least,
a mite sick.

Chastity is the greatest form of perversion.
Oscar Wilde

Slow Down,

----

slow down, from your waterfall
of feelings, intuition, and experience
with which you drown rational discourse,
which can't be conducted
by speaking from the gut.
For that's what it is;
could even be derived lower down
from the butt.

Even his ignorance is encyclopedic.
Stanislaw Jerzy Lec

Compassion,

---

in German Mitleid, more direct.
But having the same meaning in both languages,
"to suffer with."
Sympathetic pity and concern
for another's misfortunes or pain.
At best it is passive,
asking questions, listening,
trying to enter the feelings,
the agony of the other mind.
To be sensitive, to show understanding,
warmth and gentleness.
All too often the outsider, in misconstrued intent,
tries to impose on the sufferer
that which he or she perceives,
to be best in this case.
This is not compassion, empathy,
understanding, sensitivity, or warmth.
It is diagnosis at a distance,
and the distance remains.

Happiness in intelligent people is the rarest thing I know.
Ernest Hemingway

Why?

I have asked myself why women like me.
I'm no Casanova as it goes.
So, I asked one and she gave me the answer
"It is the womanly part of my mind
which seem to attract,
something most men don't possess or disclose."

There is only one happiness in life:
to love and be loved.
George Sand

Trader Joe's

No, this is not about this fine store.
But the other day I had the dubious pleasure
to sit in front of it for two hours or more
watching several hundred people
entering and leaving, doing their chore.
And what a sorry lot it was!
Most of them, slovenly dressed, hunky,
overweight, some grossly so,
few would pass as a Caucasian beau.
A dozen exceptions made the grade,
all of them women, I am afraid.
A single one had stature, taste and grace,
but, given a chance,
I'd have given her space.

When a thing is funny, search it carefully for a hidden truth.
George Bernard Shaw

Mementos

Wondering what to call my writings,
now nine volumes
of more than seventeen hundred verses,
of what I call, Poetic Prose.
What all crossed my mind,
was commemorative, keepsake, memorial,
bequest, testimonial, memorandum,
reminder, and vestige, which, at the end,
I all declined.
But as I have claimed many times before,
I write first for myself
to clear up, to state a thought,
to put down what life has wrought,
and what it still keeps ready, this juggernaut.
I settled on Mementos, because that's what most are,
reminders, souvenirs, for when I am gone
to whoever may care
to sit down to read some.

Made weak by time and fate,
but strong in will.
To strive, to seek, to find, and not to yield.
Alfred Tennyson

Local vs Global

----

thinking, that is.

The majority of people is only concerned
with what touches their lives on a local matrix.

Why wonder about what the universe is,
the kind of creatures,
except tyrannosaurus rex,
which ambled across Earth in earlier years.

Why wear masks to protect others, their peers.

Others light up their places.

None thinks of light pollution,
the stars becoming fainter,
the heavenly vault's devolution.

Some, professionally, need to reach out,
but their's is a knowledge confined to their specialty,
not what It's all about.

Ignoramus is the term for ignorant.

Too many quaver, run around, and rant,
are locally tied down,
are unable or fail to give a global perspective
it's desperately needed renown.

Suppose you succeed in breaking the wall with your head.
And what, then, will you do in the next cell?
Stanislaw Jerzy Lec

89

Scent

One of my two tall Madagascar Palms
decided to go into bloom,
an event seen only three times
in twenty-seven years.
Too clusters of large white flowers
graced the tree for a month,
exuding nightly a most pleasant scent.
Going to bed, passing near the tree,
I caught a whiff of the delicate aroma
like when a woman-of-sense,
her persona and scent having become one,
carrying it with her, passes my way.
Will I experience a fourth bloom
wafting past me in the night?

Delicacy is to affection what grace is to beauty.
Françoise d'Aubin Marquise de Maintenon

Life Goes On

Now at eighty-four I just tallied up
how many people I've known
who took their leave before me,
some older, some age-mates, some younger.
The older ones, parents and the like,
are expected not to be here any longer.
But when it comes to age mates,
and more so younger ones,
I cannot help but ponder:
What did I do right?
How lucky was I, I wonder?
A goodly dozen whom I knew
have faded into the past,
their memory becoming dimmer.
We make do with whomever is left,
their numbers becoming ever slimmer.
We, the survivors, are on a run
to briefly be remembered
while life goes on.

He who limps is still walking.
Stanislaw Jerzy Lec

91

Gosh,

----

do I wish people to be more observant,
be aware of what's going on,
what they do, what they don't, what they say.
Alas, this requires a contemplative mind,
keeping one's mouth shut,
and, gosh, open it only at the right time.

Perhaps it is better to be irresponsible and right,
than to be responsible and wrong.
Winston Churchill

Depth

Here and there, I meet a woman or man,
when after some words have been spoken,
I become aware
- it is a delight -
that I have found depth, not just a token.
Self-assured they give of themselves,
their persona, their experience, their life, their Self.
What joy it is to explore such minds.
If only there were more of their kind.

Nothing is great or little otherwise than by comparison.
Jonathan Swift

Trauma

To be deeply distressed and disturbed
requires feeling.
In battle-weary soldiers it is known as P.T.S.D.,
Post Traumatic Stress Disorder.
Emotional signs include:
sadness, fear, difficulty with relationships,
changes in appetite, depression, and anxiety,
to name a select few.
All symptoms are displayed
by my battle-weary RikkiCat
after getting into a nightfall fight
with an unknown adversary.
Slowly, she is getting out of her funk,
with me coaxing her back to normalcy.
So, here are two dissimilar creatures
with like symptoms.
What does this tell us about the ability to feel?
Dare you call this anthropomorphizing!
You did not see the behavior of my cat companion.

Selfish persons are incapable of loving others,
but they are not capable of loving themselves either.
Erich Seligmann Fromm

94

Term of Endearment

My term of endearment for my RikkiCat
is Puppie, from the German Puppe, a doll.
I am aware that it's not quite appropriate
because Puppie has claws, after all.

Where love is, no disguise can hide it for long;
where it is not. none can simulate it.
François de La Rochefoucauld

Suffering

---

is good for the growth of the soul.
Not the ethereal Christian one
but a down-to-earth homespun,
the one we must work a lifetime on.

If we desire to judge justly, we must persuade ourselves
that none of us is without sin.
Lucius Annaeus Seneca

Prediction

Up on the ledge the couple stood
likely arguing what, if anything,
of their marriage was good.
Down here, on Tamariu's rocky shore,
the surf pounding just below,
another woman shared my lore.
Audaciously, I predicted – yo,
that within a year, the woman up on the ledge
and I would be married.
Thus it came to be,
alas, not without plenty of woe.

The great question, which I have not been able to answer, is,
"What does a woman want?"
Sigmund Freud

Boulder Thoughts

Once more I sit on my favorite, sun-warmed rock.
Having lost a few pounds following surgery,
the granite boulder feels a touch harder, maybe.
Somewhere in the bushes is my companion,
my injured RikkiCat.
The afternoon sun slants through the trees,
throwing dapples of light on rocks, bushes, and d.g.
(decomposed granite)
Now, eight weeks after surgery
I ponder how my recovery will be.
At eighty-four, the operation is an expression of hope.
Bolder thoughts for a future to cope.
I'm doing great, drive, walk well,
even walk alternating steps.
Four more months and I will be at my best.
I've been warned, it will take almost a year,
but, heck, I'll do better, with a smidgeon of cheer.

It does not matter how slowly you go
so long as you you do not stop.
Confucius

Kilimanjaro

At 19,341 feet the tallest extinct African volcano,
my dream it was to climb for years.
Alas, I got to see it only from the plains of Amboseli,
its peak hidden by clouds.
It is good that I did not get to try this mountain,
as later, in my sixties, I found out,
when I climbed Mt. Humphreys at 13,883 feet,
the tallest peak of the San Francisco range.
Of my three companion mountaineers
one was older, the other two in their forties.
Halfway, the oldster gave up and went back.
Eventually, I told the youngsters to go ahead.
They made it to the peak alright
while a thunderstorm kept me short by
a few hundred feet.
Two of my fellow climbers quickly fell asleep
on the drive back to Prescott,
while I struggled mightily to stay awake.
A couple of years later I tried the mountain again,
left early, solitary, to the 9,200 feet Snowbowl.

I barely met others going up.
At the peak the wind blew fiercely,
but the view was magnificent.
Walking down, I realized it was Saturday.
A crowd of one hundred or more
was on its way up.
The final half mile my calf tendons forced me
again and again to stop.
Reaching my car I emptied my thermos of hot,
sweet, black coffee, and drove home.
Well, it hadn't been Kilimanjaro
but Mt. Humphreys I had done.

Zeal without knowledge
is fire without light.
Thomas Fuller

Kauz

Willy, my friend of many years,
just called me a "Kauz."
In German a Kauz is an owl,
but also, as in English, an oddball, it appears.
I love owls.
Why he called me an oddball
may be justified,
for I keep my mobile voice mail filled,
so that no message can be filed.
If someone wants to reach me
he or she can try again.
A technophobe I've become in my older years.
I so ken.

Better a diamond with a flaw
than a pebble without.
Dale Carnegie

Emotion

With conditions right
we learn, are taught, in early life
to quell our desires, our wants, our plights.
Social constraints can become a blight,
such as when Blacks arouse policemen's ire,
the officers responding in kind,
both caught by the force of their social bind.
We must transcend our primal spec.
It is the hallmark of civilized woman and man
to keep their emotions in check.

In a world of hunchbacks
a fine figure becomes monstrosity.
Honore de Balzac

Warmth

Every once in a while,
in the hospital, a doctor's office, or dentist,
the nurse or assistant puts a hand on my shoulder.
For just a few seconds.
And yet, how much caring, and comfort it expresses.
Ah, the warmth a human touch,
only a woman can give as such.
Hail to these women who know what it takes.

The supreme function of reason is to show man [and woman]
that some things are beyond reason.
Blaise Pascal

Emotion-driven

Virtually all my writing, my Prosetry,
is driven by emotion,
filtered by intellect, as far as I can see.
My well seems to have been well stocked,
whether by education, experiences, even DNA.
It takes something to thus reveal
what moves the writer, what he likes and dislikes,
what he thinks of the world,
and what he loves.
Hate was filtered out by the intellect.
I found it of great interest
that few, if any, of the friends
I asked for Comments on my verses,
were able or willing to express, explore,
how, if at all, my Prosetry touched them,
struck a chord.

Nothing is more conducive to peace of mind
than not having any opinion at all.
Georg Christoph Lichtenberg

104

Matter of Fact

These days, worse than opinion or conjecture,
is the rampant increase in lies, cheats, misinformation,
dishonesty, fabrication,
falsehood, and deceits.
Whatever there is of truth is shunted aside.
There is this man who said:
"We all have our own facts."
It shows what his education lacks:
We all have our opinions,
with some folk's opinion being based on facts.

Some follows get credit for being conservative
when they are only stupid.
Kin Hubbard

Alhambra

Sixty years ago, ah, young as I was,
I saw the Alhambra near Granada.
In Arabic al Hambra means The Red,
derived from the red rammed earth
of which its facade is made.
The Moorish monarchs knew how to build.
I was stunned by the interior architecture
- and still am today -
its sophistication, its esthetic beauty,
its art, its human scale,
against which the towers of today's Dubai pale.

During times of universal deceit
telling the truth becomes a revolutionary. act.
George Orwell

Wager

For the months of rehabilitation required
to recover from replacing my left knee,
I made the wager for a few more years
of unencumbered walking,
to walk once more among the forest's trees.
And, f course, to get around as I please.
But new afflictions keep popping up.
There's just no peace of mind,
except that this mind, thank the devil,
is still on the up'n'up.

On the top of each peak
you are on the edge of the abyss.
Staislaw Jerzy Lec

Sardonic

---

some of my jests have become,
because, as it stands, ever less do I give a damn.
It is, because,
the end feels ever more close.
Very close, too, is the definition below.
Sardonic is disdainfully or cynically humorous,
often scornfully mocking an uncomfortable truth,
not necessarily malicious, but skeptical
as far as it goes.
An example is when my psycho-friend
visits me, and I babble along.
He's usually quietly listening,
contributing little to the conversation.
Then I, audaciously, make the claim
that he comes visiting me only
to be entertained.

Only when we come to the end,
we decide whether the path was correct.
Paul Valery

Personhood

Ah, personhood, personality, character,
so hard to attain.
Years of work is required
to evolve and maintain,
what must be built, bit by bit,
consisting of many decisions, right and wrong,
failures, to be admitted and undone.
Not making oneself a victim,
but taking responsibility, not letting things go.
How many people have the mettle
to work on themselves,
consciously and sub-consciously,
to achieve personhood,
even if it takes a lifetime to grow.

A journey of a thousand miles
begins with a single step.
Lao Tsu

Language,

----

a living entity,
changes from Jahr zu Jahr*.
The English word "yes" is headed
for the German "ja."
It is transformed
via the American "yeah"
to the even shorter German-sounding "yah."

* year to year

Revealing

Most people keep their so-called secrets,
their innermost thoughts,
close to their hearts,
provided they even contain any worthwhile art,
thoughts about being, about life, the world,
not just mundane crap, ah well,
it rhymes, as little as a fart.
Is there a great emptiness they need to conceal?
Or are they too insecure
themselves to reveal?

I want to know what moves you, what you are looking forward to,
what brings you delight, what tugs at your heart strings, what
gets you up in the morning. I want to know about both your
dreams and your fears.
Maria Shriver

Look Out Outlook

I'm becoming ever more sardonic about life.
The great mass of people
being born, to eat, drink, fornicate, raise a few kids,
do some work, then are afraid to die.
Come to think of it:
The mask deniers think it a lie.
With barely any knowledge of the world at large,
of history, geography, climate, and science,
they use their smart phones day by day
but then are against science
which makes their lives possible,
keeps misery at bay.

The secret of man's being is not only to live,
but to have something to live for.
Fyodor Mikhallovich Dostoyevsky

Languid 2

A term which has crept into our covid times.
Fewer things need to be done right away.
We've got time on our hands.
If something's not done,
there's always another day.
The importance of tasks has slipped.
We are drifting along.
I can understand the people
who want to go out and mingle,
covid be damned.

Some like to understand what they believe in.
Others like to believe in what they understand.
Stanislaw Jerzy Lec

Solace

Can it be that mind conjured
successive afflictions to be endured?
For want of being wanted, to be understood.
Love would be too much to ask.
No, just a little bit of want to decant.
Without, slow death is ever closer at hand.
Is it that, in early times, want expressed was scant?
– not easy these times were –
It was expressed, but Touch wasn't there.
Forever longing for the warmth, the acceptance,
yet having poor knowledge of this human affair,
there remained forever this wish
to be wanted, to share.
Have I now sufficiently deep-psyched
and justified this need to be wanted?
But, for as long as it works,
I will remain undaunted.
May solace through my humor be granted.

Everything is illusion.
Even that last sentence.
Stanislaw Jerzy Lec

Light

Why do I find the beams of light
entering the rooms these afternoons
so beautifully warm and bright?
Is it just the season to be
or am I more attuned to see?
Some are small dapples, others are bold.
Ephemeral all are,
following the sun's everlasting path.
Is being aware of the sunny side
a knowing that the end is ever closer in sight?

Misery is almost always the result of thinking.
Joseph Joubert

Decisions

Life is a bunch of decisions.
Little ones and big.
Come to think of it: Life is a gig.
It is a melody of every person's run
to collect as many tunes
in their attempt a person to become.
And, baby, should you be in doubt,
trust me, this is what it's all about.

Patience is also a form of action.
Auguste Rodin

Slow Lane

Some people go quickly
by heart attack or stroke.
An accident or agressive cancer
may cut others short.
Then, others caught in the slow lane,
are dying little by little;
it is a bane.

Never saw off the branch you are on,
unless you are being hanged from it.
Stanislaw Jerzy Lec

Flirting with Death

Friends urge me not to dwell on my demise,
that another day is yet to rise.
Yes it will, one more affliction to bring.
One more to eventually do me in.
Thus I write here and there
that soon I will go.
I tease the Rim Greaper
for whatever it's worth.
That's why it is called:
Flirting with death.

The first condition for immortality is death.
Stanislaw Jerzy Lec

Safari

In Tanzania, a few years ago,
I met a Kenian couple leading a group.
She's kept in touch, here and there,
by email, as it were.
Her nickname is Mouse,
which is why I addressed her with
Dear Mus musculus,
just for the fun of it.
If only I could, I would,
join them in Kenia once more.
I must urge her to organize
a wheelchair safari,
for me to make it come true,
a final encore.

Wisdom comes by disillusionment.
Gerge Santayana

Thrift

The other day, lo and behold,
a nice middle-aged, childless couple told me
that they think they are thrifty,
when they have a house, three cars,
and every gadget in the world.
Center cut filet mignon,
pricier than the regular cut, spurned.
Then there is, once more behold,
this young couple with two children, not very old.
At minimum wage he works two shifts.
With their scant resources,
they must count every red cent,
on what to forget and on what to spend.
Forced they are to use their money
carefully, not wastefully, not swift.
How relative is the little word thrift.

The dangers gather as the treasures rise.
Samuel Johnson

Gender

Once more I feel the need to address
what one of my lady-friends claims I often express,
which is, that I love to flirt, but never in excess.
Now, hetero that I am,
I flirt with women, not with men.
This takes me back to Flirting with Death.
Since I flirt with females, not with males,
Death must be female, for all I care.
Thus I look forward to Her embrace.

If we don't know life,
how can we know death.
Confucius

Afflictions

I've added one more to my affliction palette,
angio sarcoma on top of my head.
Will these ailments never end?
Will something drastic break this trend?
Or will the pattern come to a mend?
The past fifteen years have been a pain,
with one thing after another,
an unbroken chain.
Twenty-five afflictions, large and small.
A failure of function common to all.
By now I take this with a lighter heart,
waiting and wondering when another will start.
If nothing truly serious will get me to croak,
I may collect another ten disorders
during the five, six years I have given myself
to this, my life's ongoing joke.
I can only hope that what's yet to come,
I will have the guts not to succumb.

The hidden harmony is better than the obvious.
Pablo Picasso

Insecurity

---

be damned for the talent it has hemmed.
No matter its origin or cause,
what counts is overcoming its flaws.
Some people struggle their entire life
with self-doubt sub-surface ever rife.
Others grab the ox by its horn,
find ways to overcome this thorn.
Control of one's life and others, too,
provides a resemblance of security.
Beyond life's ever unknown exigencies lies
the self-confidence to deal with them as they arise.

We know our friends by their defects
rather than by their merits.
William Somerset Maugham

Victimhood

To blame someone else is easy
for whatever happened to you.
To take responsibility for what you did,
and what you did not,
shows character and personhood.

It is never too late to be
what you might have been.
George Eliot

Control 1

For some people control is a dirty word.
They viscerally associate it with everything bad.
Yet, what is worth more
than having control of one's life?
I wonder whether those rejecting such control
are truly content or is chaos rife.

One mustn't look at the abyss, because there is
at the bottom an inexpressible charm which attracts us.
Gustave Flaubert

A Full Life

Can I claim to have had a full life?
To have had children and a good wife?
To have fallen up the ladder
with an eighth-grade education
to become managing director,
successfully directing the affairs of the affiliate
of a German company across the USA.
In due course acquiring a BA in anthropology.
I had no desire to become a specialist.
My goal was to be a generalist.
Short of mathematics
I knew enough arithmetic to become a millionaire.
I have traveled the world to places galore.
Translated numerous books,
wrote a biography and poetic poetry,
not to forget the autobiography, and more.
Now, that life comes ever closer to its end
I am happy to say: I am content.
And were my wife still living by my side
I would be even more contenter.

There are more people who wish to be loved
than there are who are willing to love.
Nicolas de Chamfort

RikkiCat

----

and I, like a good husband and wife,
read each other, on our walk through life.
Right now she lies content in front of me,
stretched out on my desk,
ready for an occasional caressing treat.
The encroaching sun would heat her feet
if I had not covered them with a paper sheet.
We are companions,
telling each other what we need.
My God, what is going to happen to her
when I will need to take my leave,
so bittersweet?

A man dies as often as he loses his friends.
Francis Bacon

Also a Cat?
H.W.

Addiction

I never smoked,
nor did the real hard stuff.
I could take oxycodone
and stop it when it was enough.
Coffee and alcohol
I enjoyed in good measure.
And when it was called for
I dropped imbibing this treasure.
Chocolate never became rife.
And while I may have been physiologically lucky,
my addiction became –
to stay in control of my life.

Lying to ourselves is more deeply ingrained
than lying to others.
Fyodor Mikhailovich Dostoyevsky

Rushing Waters

With rapt attention I have gazed at rushing waters,
rapids, and waterfalls, in the course of time.
I observed and wondered about Asian tourists
walking from their bus to a site,
took a picture, turned, and left it behind.
Is this a sign of a vacuous mind?

Nothing is endless but inanity.
Johann Wolfgang von Goethe

Option

When I opted to have my left knee replaced
at the ripe old age of almost eighty-four,
I figured it would enable me
to securely walk once more.
To tread uneven ground;
to walk under the forest's trees,
and, "God-willing," for maybe five or six years.
The God-quote need not cause you fears.
Now, that the angio sarcoma has come to roost,
I must give my immune system a boost,
or my intended six year span will be deuced.
Aw shucks. Two or three years,
also seven or eight, are just as good!

Doubt is not a pleasant condition,
but certainty is an absurd one.
Voltaire

Zeal

When I wrote the biography
of my wife's missionary grandparents and parents,
I came across their mentioning of
the bioluminescence at night on an ocean crossing,
missing that the constellations appear upside down
once one approaches the equator.
That the southern sky
has fewer significant constellations,
yet the Southern Cross is never mentioned.
There are the noisy monkeys in the jungle,
a comet observed for a time.
While they introduced new vegetables and fruit
and propagation methods to the Batak natives,
the only animals repeatedly mentioned
are tigers and snakes,
creatures which threatened their lives.

Never did I find any inquiry into
what bioluminescence is, or the names of monkeys,
gibbons, macaques, maybe even orang utans,
nor that the comet was Halley's.
They certainly lived a rich life of faith,
yet the other rich life of Earth
was ignored in their missionary zeal.

You can change your faith without changing gods.
And vice versa.
Stanislaw Jerzy Lec

Flesh

Life lives off life,
a fact, for ethics not to enter.
By human yardsticks
some such consumptions in Nature
are horrific to ponder.
Ethically, nothing is wrong
for us humans to consume meat.
What has made it ethically questionable
is the industrial production of it,
the result of our increasing numbers and wealth,
and our separation from Nature.
Mind you, if ever we could arrive at the point
when we no longer need consume – unlikely –
the flesh of our fellow-creatures,
it would constitute a truly humane accomplishment.

I fear the day that technology will surpass
our human interaction.
The world will have a generation of idiots.
Albert Einstein

Intimate

My psycho-friend Norm,
my most intimate friend,
has come up with a Comment.
Short as it is, it is very well penned.
In many a conversation we probed existence,
from the simple to the grand.
He knows what he's saying,
becoming socratic, even wise.
His Comment is brief:
"Herbert lives the examined life."

Who would venture upon the journey of life,
if compelled to begin it at the end?
Françoise d'Aubigne Marquise de Maintenon

Limitations

I know my limitations,
I'm aware where I fall short,
I'm sure I know my deficits,
I need not to purport.

Man is the only creature
that refuses to be what he is.
Albert Camus

Cogitation

Desirous in many a situation.
Sadly missing in any demonstration.
Short in most human conversation.
Called for in husband and wife relation.
Even with it, beware of a false conclusion.

Believe only half of what you see
and nothing that you hear.
Edgar Allan Poe

Taking Care

It has been my call to take care of things.
How this transpired I am not quite sure.
Come to think of it, it likely came to be,
taking care of myself must've been the need.
I organized and often took charge.
Some of my fellow beings were glad of it,
for others it was too much.

If you wish to be loved, show more of your faults
than your virtues.
Edward George Bulwer-Lytton

Anthropos

No matter his or her color,
no mater where they are from,
what matters is competence
and more so good will.

We are sinful not merely because we have eaten
from the tree of knowledge,
but also because we have not eaten from the tree of life.
Franz Kafka

Pithy

I return again to my "Intimate" verse,
to elaborate about the Examined Life.
It took Norm awhile, my pithy friend,
but it was worth the wait for what he penned.
Psychologist and philosopher that he is,
he subtly changed Socrates's dictum:
"The unexamined life is not worth living,"
to my personal status:
"Herbert lives the examined life."
The insight Norm shows into my very being,
the compliment, the honor, he bestowed,
will accompany me forever,
allowing me to leave in peace.
For, after examining myself,
I try to get my readers to act likewise.
like my ancient advisor, Socrates
advised the youth of his time.
Like him, I am condemned to death,
by an evil spirit haunting my health.
Were I only able to drink from the chalice,
to join him to where we came from - earth.

The greater the dark, the easier to be a star.
Stanislaw Jerzy Lec

Elevation

Is there an evil entity which keeps us under its spell,
to grope our way higher from mere animal?
Do we need ten thousand more years
to free ourselves from its spiteful hell?
Delve into your being my hurried friends,
beyond your daily needs.
Go, broaden your perspective what life is about,
and apply it with reason and compassion,
trust, yet be skeptical, and justifiably doubt.

Is it progress if a cannibal uses a fork?
Stanislaw Jerzy Lec

Darwinian Selection

To wear or not to wear a covid mask
is not a question.
For those who refuse to wear one
for political reasons,
conservatives that they are,
it becomes a question of Darwinian selection.
In the name of freedom, the name of choice,
they don't give a damn about the death rate's rise.
Survival of the fittest, here the most intelligent,
will likely reduce the number
of conservative no-mask wearers.
A gain of scientific acumen for the nation.
I have been called cynical for suggesting this trend,
but, heck, facts is fact,
trust me, my friend.

Wherever there is uncertainty there has got to be judgement.
And wherever there is judgement there is an opportunity for
human fallibility.
Don Redelmeier

Story Tellers

Our world, our cultures, of stories are made.

Most are ancient but new ones we create.

People are raised with them from birth.

Few are aware that they live by stories we've created,

without them we would not be human,

but mere animals wand'ring the Earth.

However, the point is that all sprang

from man's fertile mind.

They are nothing but stories of whatever kind,

different from culture to culture,

by religions defined,

their adherents unaware of thus being confined.

More stories are yet to come;

others abandoned, left behind.

If one is seeking for Heaven on Earth,
has slept in geography class.
Stanislaw Jerzy Lec

Success & Luck

For success we need to make an effort.
Luck, when it crosses our path,
we need to catch by its tail.
If love can be added to the two
the three will make quite a tale.

We must believe in luck. For how else can we explain
the success of those we don't like.
Jean Cocteau

Fate

----

has decreed, based on my PET scan's read,
that, with as yet, no cancer spread,
I may hang on a while longer
to enjoy experiencing more afflictions yet.

We are more closely connected to the invisible
than to the visible.
Novalis

Anticipation

Running a business for thirty years
I've learned looking ahead for what might occur.
Annual forecasts thus common were.
For life, in general, it is good to know
what might or might not become part of the show.
It also pays to know the options one has.
If things turn out different,
well, then one changes one's path.
Anticipation isn't a solitary goal,
and beware, when it gives the illusion of control.

It is a statistical fact that the wicked work harder
to reach hell than the righteous do to enter heaven.
Henry Wheeler Shaw

Control 2

I have decided, once and for all,
to no longer try to control
financial and organizational matters
beyond my life's role.
Be this the function and pleasure
of those who follow.

Lead me not into temptation.
I can find the way myself.
Mae West

Love Me

There is Rikki, waiting on my desk,
for me to sit down
to love her, to hold and caress,
something she's done for days.
Happy I am to oblige, I confess.

You can give without loving,
but you can never love without giving.
Robert Louis Stevenson

Loss

I've never lost anything in my life,
except a mattress, a gust of wind blew off
the top of a houseboat on Lake Powell
in the midst of night.
But, come to think of it,
there is my wife.

The qualities, which a man seeks in his beloved,
are those characteristics of his own soul,
whether he knows it or not.
Plato

Personality

The sum total of an individual's qualities
form his or her distinctive character,
her nature, his temperament,
her persona, his psyche.
Yet, some people have more than others,
some display instant appeal, others turn off.
The majority is easy to doff.
A final word about the mammals we are,
Rikki, my cat, has personality, too.
A disposition of her very own.

Character is higher than intellect ...
A great soul will be strong to live,
as well as to think.
Ralph Waldo Emerson

Grudge

I've arrived at the insight
that it's not worth carrying a grudge.
It diminishes me, it's just a fudge.
I rather let go, for the time is short.
Soon everything will be gone,
so, what was it all for?

It is a part of good breeding that a man
should be polite even to himself.
Jean Paul Richter

Churning

My mind churns, as it often does
at night when I want to sleep.
It churns about what is and what was.
I reminisce, I project, I regret, I rejoice,
or get up to write a verse,
as I did in the past.
The last two surgeries seem to keep me awake,
but no, my demise is not at stake.
At times I need a narcotic pill,
but never past two in the night.
By morning I always feel alright.
Dependency is not my kind.

We promise according to our hopes
and perform according to our fears.
François de La Rochefoucauld

Plate Tectonics

You folks who pine about mankind wreaking havoc
onto our beautiful Earth,
relax, ye worriers, your concerns are for naught,
what will be will be or, maybe, not.
Look forward to another rebirth,
my daughters and sons,
but you won't be around for it to come.
A few hundred million years it will take
and then some.
The plates will be shifting,
subduction subsuming what we have wrought.
The Earth will be cleansed for a different life,
likely, but maybe not.
For the sun's heat is waxing,
thus, for life as we know it,
it will be too hot.

God gives all men all Earth to love,
But since man's heart is small,
Ordains for each one spot shall prove,
Beloved over all.
Rudyard Kipling

152

Ailments

I am a collector of ailments.
Twenty-five in a fifteen year span.
Small and large as they have been,
none have succeeded to do me in,
thanks to the good doctors of medicine.
Angio sarcoma, my latest acquisition,
is likely to stop me, at last.
But for it to succeed,
I'm certain of it,
I'll collect five more ailments
before the die is finally cast.

Life decreases in direct proportion to the force of desire.
Honore de Balzac

The Last Safari

Five years ago, in Tanzania,
I met a British-Kenyan couple,
safari company owners,
and we stayed in intermittent touch.
I told Alexandra, nicknamed Mouse,
that a final safari was my wish,
especially walking through the bush.
Alas, this, my health no longer permits.
So I told her, I am so sorry:
"I'll only come for a wheelchair safari."

The future is not what it used to be.
Paul Valery

Believe It, Or Not

I have a patent for a mask
with a trap door, and little lever,
to open and shut.
It enables the wearer to eat
and to chat.
It's available on Amazon
for twenty-nine ninety-five,
with all proceeds going to charity.
Trust me, this ain't no jive.

The most dangerous untruths
are truths slightly distorted.
Georg Christoph Lichtenberg

Trust Me Not

I kid a lot,
which is why I've warned my friends
To trust me not!
But warned them too to know enough
when, for once, it's not a bluff.

Tirade

A tirade justifies
that which one knows isn't right.
Defensiveness isn't far behind.
A sense of wrongness
will keep gnawing on the speaker's mind.
If not, it shows the person is blind.

The things we remember best
are those better forgotten.
Baltasar Gracian

Unicorn

There, right in front of my forehead
the sarcoma appeared slightly offset.
But might it be something else that I've been beset?
The way I have been pictured by a few folks I met,
it may very well be the growth of a horn.
However, two horns, the devil's head adorn.
I would be one short, or may two more yet grow?
But if it's only one it would certainly show
that I was only half the devil
through the years, long ago.

Half the work that is done in the world
is to make things appear what they are not.
E.R. Beadle

Tragedy

My sarcoma's been called a tragedy,
but, per se, an illness a tragedy is not.
A tragedy is the unhappy ending
of the afflicted life's lot.

Nostalgia is a seductive liar.
George W. Ball

Anecdotal

A lot which people in conversations spout
is anecdotal, subject to doubt,
unreliable, unscientific, To be trusted is a greater
compliment personal accounts.
And on stuff like this, opinions, not facts,
people, by a large measure,
run their lives as if they count.

Talk sense to a fool
and he calls you foolish.
Euripides

Promises

Some folks make promises
they know they won't keep.
Others let them go asleep.
Some do forget, some overreached,
the honor to keep their word
was surely breached.

To be trusted is a greater compliment
than to be loved.
George MacDonald

Memory Aids

I've had a tough time recalling "Dillards," the store,
until "dill," my favorite herb, came to the fore.
For "anecdotal," I had to go farther ashore,
to Anak Krakatoa, the "child"
the volcano Krakatoa bore.
Oh, could I only come up with a memory aid
for every name, for every word,
becoming a temporary fugitive ,
when in a conversation in need.
Alas, my memory's no longer that good
that I could recall all these memory aids
as I wish, I could.

He who doesn't lose his wits over certain things
has no wits to lose.
Gotthold Lessing
Laughs

Laughs

I take pleasure in getting people to laugh,
but entertainer I am not.
These times, with covid rampant,
telephone chats are what we mostly got.
With a few of my friends I laugh a lot,
me twisting the meaning of words
of our conversation, sometimes more often,
than I ought.
But there are a some others
with whom my jests remain little or naught.

Eccentricity is one of the hallmarks
of strong characters and original minds.
Andrew Garve

Vaccinations

Having been born in CE1936,
I collected a few vaccinations,
when infectious diseases were yet of a hefty mix.
There was pertussis, diphtheria,
measles, mumps, and rubella, chickenpox,
even smallpox still,
whopping cough, polio, diphtheria, and tetanus,
shingles, and not to forget the flu.
Malaria pills as a prophylactic for the tropics,
and a yellow fever stab I got too.
Gosh, the protection I and my contemporaries got.
We never questioned the vaccines' safety.
Science and technology were thought to be good.
The Contergan calamity brought a change of mood
when babies were born without arm, leg, or foot.
Today, with a better educated public,
skepticism, even fear of vaccination has grown.
Life without inoculation has become unknown.
Ignorance, superstition, and fear
will yet drag us down
for this plethora of diseases to recur.

No snowflake in an avalanche feels responsible.
Stanislaw Jerzy Lec

Pictures

I have been on several safaris.
My wife took pictures.
I did not.
In Tanzania, five years ago,
on my solo last safari,
I didn't take a single shot.
I looked, I saw, I remember, I forgot.

How do I know what I think
till I have written it down.
Oswald Veblen

Cacophony

For lack of a better word I call it that,
Titter, Facebook, TikTok, and such.
A harsh, discordant mix
of images, words, and sounds.
A din, a racket, a dissonance,
better still, a caterwauling of opinions,
emotions, that is.
Even the Internet has largely come to this.
By the wayside largely have gone facts.
What good will these electronic media
with their mostly sentiment-based cacophony do us?

"You see how I try
To reach with words
What matters most
And how I fail."
Czeslaw Milosz

Scylla and Charybdis,

the two monsters Odysseus had too pass
in his wanderings at the Strait of Messina.
The American synonyms being:
"Being between a rock and a hard place,"
or "Between the devil and the deep blue sea."
Well, I'm between all three.
I need exercise, but doing it,
swells up my replaced knee.

There are no whole truths; all truths are half-truths.
It is trying to treat them as whole truth that plays the devil.
Alfred North Whitehead

Modicum

A smidgen of affection and companionship
seemed to still exist through the years.
Now I must realize that both
have been transferred in toto to someone else,
nothing is left at this watershed,
just when life hangs by a thick thread.

Everyone must be who he was in the first years of his life,
even if later these were buried under.
No one can become what he cannot find in his memories.
Jean Améry

Justification

Our desires, our needs determine our acts.
I know this all too well.
We create a new reality.
The old one we forget
and find justification for what we did.
Yet, in some people there remains this little voice
which ever so softly reminds:
"Your new reality is of the wrong kind."

So convenient a thing it is to be a rational creature, since it
enables us to find or make a reason for every thing
one has a mind to do.
Benjamin Franklin

Unlove

One can love someone for what has been,
and unlove the same for what is?
Circumstances call for this.
Or should one just stick with love
for better or worse?

As one grows older one becomes wiser
and more foolish.
François de La Rochefoucauld

Acceptance

There comes a time in a couple's life,
when wanting the other
– I'm not speaking of love –
is no longer alive.
Deficits become magnified
and, what once drew them together
withers and dies,
until nothing is left
– it may take decades of time –
not until death does part us,
but when it becomes convenient,
when a better satisfier of needs is found,
and the other,
who hung on for life, is now hell-bound.

I should not talk so much about myself
if there were anybody else whom I knew as well.
Henry David Thoreau

Shame

----

is that little voice in the back of the head
reminding the perpetrator
of a wrong or foolish behavior,
an act committed,
that not all is hunky-dory
no matter how he or she sees it.
But then, some folks have no shame to admit.

Morality, like art, means drawing a line someplace.
Oscar Wilde

Stamina

In my teens I was tops at the hundred meter dash,
at longer distances not so much.
In my forties canoe trips tested my strength
with portages of varying lengths.
At fifty-five, in nineteen-ninety-two
we made Prescott our home,
and soon, up and down the hills we roamed.
In time the hills no longer called,
my energy had faded, stalled.
Sessile computer work took its place,
translations, mind tasks, were embraced.
At the time refractory anemia was diagnosed.
Nothing was done about it,
until in two-thousand eighteen I almost croaked.
Hemoglobin had dropped below its hold,
a pacemaker was installed;
my departure had been stalled.
Treated for hemolytic anemia I was stabilized.
While this was done Meniere's disease
kept me at times immobilized.

It's best I quit here, I could go on,
with all the afflictions,
twenty-five in fifteen years,
I was kept on the run. Is there time left
to collect yet some?

Radiation

For five weeks to come
my lesion on top of my head
will receive five-days-a-week radiation,
permanently killing the hair at this location.
To compensate for the loss on top
I thought to grow a beard
making up for it.
Humor me,
I think I will likely look like a shile of pit.

It is unhealthy to live.
He who lives dies.
Stanislaw Jerzy Lec

Retrospect

Six decades ago, young and naive,
we promised each other
for the coming years
to be faithful, yet, should the situation arise,
we could have an outside physical relation,
but not one of the mind.
Alas, this was sixty years ago,
when, we were unable to conceive
what might come yet to be,
while we were still young and naive.

After enlightenment, the laundry.
Henry Wheeler Shaw

Driven

Once I had outgrown my dormant pre-teens,
I aimed to excel in life's multifarious scenes.
Dynamic, I went for what I took into sight.
I was tops in drafting,
sold goods to make a buck,
and itched to travel,
which took me to Scandinavia,
Africa, France, Spain, and back.
I gained a wife, three children, too,
had a well-paying job,
but longed to see more of the world.
With the consent of my wife
Canada called, then the United States.
I survived the discharge of my colleagues,
fell up the ladder as managing director,
to rebuild the company in the coming years.
Through tumultuous times I stayed engaged,
eventually importing and selling myself.
And in due course acquired wealth.
I facilitated courses in history and science,
traveled to countries across the world.

A dining group I kept on track,
just as I did with another discussing
what makes the world tick.
I translated and wrote many a work,
in due course, in American language, I excelled.
And yet, and yet,
as the years did pass, depressed I was
wanting acceptance instead of rejection,
at a loss of how to be loved.
Until, in early two-thousand-eighteen, at last,
my oxygen-starved mind and heart,
the deficit of hemoglobin,
caused me to almost depart.
Now, I have come to the end.
Success came my way,
I worked for it.
Driven, I was,
and I payed for it,
in issues of health,
and the wife I beheld.

There are no secrets which do not permit
themselves to be told.
Edgar Allan Poe

Enough

I will quit rambling,
enough is enough.
Only one thing is left
I wish the bereft:
That you find what you need,
in the years you have left
of which I wasn't blessed.
Let me say it once more:
Enough is enough.
But what remains to wonder is:
What is love?

There are more people who wish to be loved
than there are who are willing to love.
Nicolas de Chamfort

Part II

Comments on one or more volumes of my Poetic Prose:

I believe that every writer would like to learn how his writings are being received by his readers. Some friends volunteered comments.
It occurred to me to ask several others to "come out of the bushes" and let me have their thoughts. This is why I sent out the below email hoping for more input.

Greetings, Friends!
By now I have self-published eight volumes with roughly 1700 verses of, what I call, my Poetic Prose.
From many recipients of my handed-out books I have never received a word of what they think of my scribbles. But I would like to find out more of how I come across.
However, in the course of time, several of my reader-friends have sent me brief impressions about how my writings struck them, what they meant to them, how they saw them. Often, the accompanying aphorisms tickled them more than my preceding verse.
The thought occurred to me to include a selection of such Comments – I'm not looking for plaudits – in my ninth volume. It is my intention to show the names of the respondents if permitted.
Following are (two) examples of comments I have received. I would greatly appreciate receiving yours. Thank you very much.
Herbert

"I am glad I read them slowly, perhaps one poem every evening. Some are so powerful and profound they sometimes affect my dreams."
John Haupt

Dear friend, Herbert,
I was delighted to find a copy of your (latests) book on my doorstep. Thank you, thank you. Fortunately, I have had time this afternoon to read some, and skim some of its innards, and have enjoyed them all. There is something magical in the way you tell your stories, honor your friends, create your poems. Maybe it's not exactly magical, maybe it's also the love that spills over and through your many well-chosen words. In all, I enjoy your willingness to share fully who you are. You tell a complete story, and one can walk away saying, "I really know this man and like what I see." Your book is a treasure, and I will look forward to picking it up from time and time and saying, "Hi, Herbert, I remember this poem.
Zene Krogh

I've been meaning to tell you, Herbert, how much I treasure your latest book of poems. I especially enjoy the nature poems along with Ute's lovely cover photograph. My favorites, though, have been like "Pithy" - the shorter ones. It is obvious that maturity and illnesses have brought you compassion and understanding which gives your poems a universal appeal. Thank you, too, for including those unusual quotations which I have appreciated. The haiku at the end is lots of fun, too. *Thoughts* is a little gem which I keep by my reading lamp so I can pick it up and browse at odd moments during the day or evening.
You are truly an inspired poet and I thank you for sharing your *Thoughts* with Fulton and me.
Nancy Wright

Also, I wanted to tell you that I am finding *"Searching,"* your newest volume of "poetic prose" delightful. With the beautiful poems, the bits of humor, the appropriate aphorisms, and the various African pieces, it is truly a gem. Thank you.
Nancy Wright

I am most taken by Herb's unique and wondrous use of the English language. Not being a native English speaker, Herb utilizes the language in a most creative, effective manner. Beyond the mechanics of the language, Herb has what might be termed a free-flowing interest in an unending list of disparate topics. Many are prompted by a recent experience, a current event, a turn in the weather, a frenetic or acrobatic move by his cat. When one opens his latest volume, one can expect to learn, to share, to be amazed at the scope of his interests. Herb can be melancholy, whimsical, morose and elated all in a few pages of his work. His educated musings provoke thought, bring smiles to one's face and, frequently, evoke personal introspection. I am always entertained and educated by his work. I await the next volume.........
Bob Greninger

Kudos to Herb Windolf for his series of thought-provoking books
When one bares one's soul, as you often do in your poems, you allow your reader a glimpse into your mind, your soul and your heart. This is indeed a special talent and a frame of mind to be willing to expose the inner self. It is truly a gift to your friends as a way to know and understand you better. Your subject matter reveals your passions - the "rightness' of things, your pet, nature, geology, the universe and human connections. Keep composing!!!
Marcia Cossaboom

Hi Herb,

Looking through your books, I am constantly amazed at the wide range of subject matter. Along with the wide range, I am impressed with the profundity of your observations. They show a very active mind and soul at work.

Marian Powell

Herb,

The book "*Searching*" itself is simply beautiful, lush, professional, a pleasure to gaze upon and to hold. Despite our very long friendship, I've learned more about you, your background and accomplishments in the first five minutes of reading than I have in all these years.

You call your work "Poetic Prose", but I find it more descriptive to say that it is somewhat of a stream of consciousness, and certainly philosophic in tone.

That is to say, you express in the gentle meanderings of your mind how you view the world and its inhabitants. Viz: Herb Windolf, PHD.

As I wend my way through your thoughts as expressed in prose/poetry, Herb, I'm struck with admiration at the extent of your English vocabulary.

Of course, you've lived in this country for ages, yet having such a command of English word-smithing *in a second language*, is truly impressive.

I'm enjoying the depth and diversity of your texts, absorbing your ideas that are sometimes dark and concerning, other times seeing the tongue-in-cheek humor that has long defined you.

Your friend

Herbert,

as a recipient of your mental exercises and your efforts to present everyday's life in a manner that has me make an effort to understand your interpretation of "matters", I say thank you for letting me be part of your deep philosophical thoughts. I do not always share your ideas, nor have I

always read all your outpourings, but they do give me reason to pause and reflect, for which I say ; Thank you
Willy Liesner

Herbert,
In response to your request, I have thought long about what I want to convey. Besides admiring your ability to express yourself well and interestingly, I think I have enjoyed most seeing your personal evolution through these books. It made me think back to the first time we got acquainted at our studio. Small doses of each other over those years grew to a friendship I value. Your writings spoke, revealing a breadth I could not have known otherwise. Then as we have grown older, your poems expressing those changes, sadder, wiser, wistful, playful, too. Thank goodness for your cat! I enjoy reading between the lines, because I know you and care about you. So keep writing, as many of us await the "next chapter" of your life laid before us, to share from each of our perspectives.
Cathy Krieger

One of my favorite poems written by Herbert Windolf is "Infinity". It reflects the realistic nature of many of Herb's poems. Our human 'life cycle' and our oneness with nature are so well stated in the poem. I am very grateful to have contemplated and enjoyed so many of Herb's poems.
Matthew Lukaszewski

Herbert,
You have been one of my closest friends for over 40 years and we have weathered together many different life experiences over those years. Your poetry has given me a clear picture of your inner thoughts and how they reflect back on my life.
Paul Sipiera

Hi Herbert,

Here I go:

"When I first read Herb Windolf's poetic words, my heart smiled. Here was a man who had learned to express what I sometimes struggle to put down on paper, all the while thinking it in my head. Both the trivial and deeply meaningful observations make for a rich life that has obviously been well and deeply lived. While Herb and I draw very different conclusions on a number of ponderings about life's deeper meaning, I find myself going back time and again to his books to pull out one nugget or another that speaks to me that day. I appreciate the seasonings of his now eight decades plus of human insight."

Bussis,

Elke Speliopoulos

Dear Herb,

I've have enjoyed your thoughts and reflections over the years. Thanks much for passing them along.

As you know, I was not too long ago paid for my own thoughts and knowledge   as I passed them on to students, colleagues, and decision-makers of varying persuasions and positions.

Your thinking tends to be more reflective, more philosophically-oriented than my thinking. It's about as fact-based, but of a different dimension, of varying degrees of profundity. Your thinking tends less to specifics than mine.

I also think your books of poetic prose reflect something of you. I look for you in the foci and the implicit analysis. I think I find your thoughts, your concerns, your conclusions.

As you know, I frequently agree with both focus and explanation.

Please produce another round when the spirit strikes. It's good for you. And for me/us.

Appreciative Abrazos,

Ed Williams

Hello Herbert,

my knowledge of the English language limits my ability to say much about the form of your writing, which is why I look at

your poems as a psychologist, asking myself "who is the other and what purpose his actions have." Your poems show a broad-based interest, considerations of manifold subjects. Putting them in writing, you establish your own world of thought. Beyond this,

I imagine that this kind of writing can become an act of psycho-hygenics, a good way to meet oneself, to get to know oneself better.

Greetings,

Dörthe Rutkowsky

Translated from German and edited by H.W.

Herbert
lives the examined life*
Norm Gordon

* Socrates

"The unexamined life is not worth living" is a famous dictum apparently uttered by Socrates at his trial for impiety and corrupting youth, for which he was subsequently sentenced to death, as described in Plato's Apology (38a5–6).

My most intimate friend, Norm Gordon, PhD in psychology, whom I call my psycho-friend in jest, has come up with the briefest Comment of all. While he does not reveal details of how my poetic prose has affected him, he demonstrates a tremendous insight into my being, the result of years of conversations on a multitude of subjects and interactions.
I feel honored.

Part III

Introduction
to the below Autobiography

Through the months of November and December 2004, until the end of January 2005, the time of the great Indian Ocean tsunami, I wrote the bulk of the following autobiography. In subsequent months I added a passage, here and there, when some items surfaced in my memory.

By 2011, after entered a few occurred events and thoughts, further entries petered out. Further autobiographical comments were from thereon represented by my poetic writing which, in later years I named Poetic Prose, even Prosetry, a word I coined.

I self-published these largely autobiographical verses in eight volumes, titled Observations and Reflection, Otherwise, Pondering, Musings, Contemplations, Thoughts, Searching, and Shadows and Light. A ninth book is in gestation. After my first publication, Observations and Reflections, I thought no further publications would be following. Often, I said: This is the last one, not expecting to have the time for expressing additional ideas and memories. Friends scoffed and teased me about my negative outlook. They were correct.

What I try to express in my poetic prose, usually factual, sometimes poetic, are memories, ideas, contemporary reports and comments of concern to me. They are most certainly autobiographical and complement my autobiography.

A number of great thinkers have influenced my mind. They include Charles Darwin, Michel de.Montaigne, Richard Feynman, and Abraham Maslow. My friend Norman

Gordon introduced me to the latter for which I am immensely grateful. Maslow, one of the founders of humanistic psychology, in the 1950s introduced the Hierarchy of Needs, and Self-actualization in the search for personal growth. Maslow helped putting me on the path of pursuing Sophia, a never ending task.

Prescott, AZ   2021

Remembrances
and
Interpretations

Autobiography

of Herbert Windolf

1936 to 2021

Contents

1. Why and how

My daughter, Kirsten, recently asked me to write down the way I came to be, or rather how I wended my way through life – up to this point. Her thoughts were, that it would help to understand how my children were affected by these events. And since this was the fourth request for my biographical notes, and I am now also sixty eight years old, I figure it may be okay to do so.

I will attempt to be as truthful as possible, although I must say, that my interpretations on how some of my idiosyncrasies evolved and played themselves out, may be subject to my subjectivity. The same holds true for my interpretations of the personalities of some of the family members, friends, superiors, acquaintances, and other people who crossed my path and influenced me, contributed to who I became.

When I began writing during the first half of December of 2004, I stuck more or less to my immediate experiences. Then, Karen had given me as a present the Memoirs of Amos Oz, an Israeli writer, called Tales of Love and Darkness. And while I am by far not a writer of his talent, I took from him the idea of entering, adding all kinds of peripheral experiences, which I am still engaged with this February of 2005.

2. Family Background

First, I feel to have to go back in time from where my immediate forebears came from. Let me begin with my mother's background. Her mother, my maternal grandmother, was born in Jagsthausen, a small agricultural village in Swabia. Oh, let me inject something here. Jagsthausen holds the castle of the Berlichingens. One of the Berlichingens' ancestors is credited to have rejected emperor Charles the Fifth troops' request of surrender during the Thirty Years War by showing his bare butt through a castle window, telling the emperor's emissary to lick (not kiss, as Anglo-Saxons say) his arse. Maybe some of my irreverence comes from that. More about this later.

I do not know much about how Marie Luise Rohleder, who was born on Dec. 1, 1879, met her husband to be, Jakob Michels, a baker by trade, to marry him on July 28, 1904. She had been a household employee with an upper class family, and when she intended to marry, this family (a daughter of which later became the wife of Germany's first post-WW2 chancellor, Konrad Adenauer) extended a loan to the newlyweds, enabling them to start a bakery and grocery store. The marriage produced a boy and two daughters. My mother Karoline, being the youngest, was born on Sept. 30, 1908. In 1924 her father died from the effects of a WW1 injury. While the two older siblings went their respective ways, my mother, at age 16, had to help her widowed mother to run the grocery store to support the family. The bakery was brought to a halt. With only a couple of years break Mama, my mother, stood in this store for the rest of her life until she retired, closing the store. Oma, her mother, I remember making Spätzle, Swabian handmade noodles, over simmering water, scraping the viscous dough from a board into the suds. Much, much later I have done the same, when we wanted to introduce Prescott friends to this very southern German dish. Oma died of a stroke in her mid-sixties when a brother of hers showed up in Biebrich, for whatever reasons against her wishes. The excitement it caused seemed to have been the reason for the event. She lost her ability to speak. Later I was present in the room were she lay in bed, when she was given pencil and paper to write down what she could not say. Her hand did no longer provide the

195

control to do even this. The next day, January 19, 1951 at age 72, she was dead!

My paternal grandmother, Johanna Karoline Wilhelmine Rosine Windolf, grew up with two brothers. One became a castle custodian, the other a locksmith. I always remember Johanna as a strong-willed woman. On Nov. 10, 1906 she gave birth to a son, Hans Sebastian, carrying the mother's name. I had known, that her family's name had been Windolf. I may have been around ten years of age, when I became aware of the discrepancy. How could my father's name be Windolf, when his mother's family name had been Windolf! Innocent as I was at that age, I must have dropped a word somehow. That's when my mother took me aside one day and explained it to me in a kind of hush-hush tone. Supposedly the father had been killed in an early car accident in Mainz. It was a blemish, social stigma still attached at the time.

Father's mother then raised her son, in what must have been some dire circumstances, by knitting dresses, etc. for paying customers. Thus my father grew up without knowing a father under the tutelage of a tough woman. Johanna and her son lived for an unknown number of years in the Schlossstraße in Biebrich, right next to the maintenance yard of the chateau, in a house which has long since been torn down. When you look at the charcoal and watercolor picture I much later purchased from my girlfriend's mother, Margarete Tuberg-Gundelach, it was a house adjoining the one on the very left. I gave the painting to my father as a birthday present. At the time of my father's childhood it was a decrepit neighborhood, today it is all fixed up. The two must have been church-mouse poor! That's why never a word was lost of that time. It is unknown to me when they moved out there to Elisabethenstraße 1, whether this was before my parents married and put running water and electric power in there or already before. Omi died in her sleep on February 9, 1950 at age 66 from a heart attack after having been put through a regimen to lose weight.

Both houses, Elisabethenstr. 1 and Rheingaustr. 150, my mother's folks home, had been built around 1750, and were, maybe, a hundred meters apart. Just as my uncle Fritz, mother's brother, my father went to engineering school, my uncle studying electrical, my father mechanical engineering. While Papa, my father, was unemployed for a year during the twenties, he, as well as my mother's family did advance into, what I would call, lower middle class. This was the time when families hoped and worked for their children's advance up the social ladder, something only immigrants seem to bring any longer to Western societies these days.

The hygienic facilities, washing clothes and oneself, were, compared to today, very poor. While there was a bathtub at Elisabethenstraße, there was no water heater. Bath water had to be heated on a stove! At Rheingaustraße a bathroom was installed after Oma had died. It held a bathtub and a coal-fired water heater. Years later it was converted to gas-heating – a great improvement.

Clothing, shirts, underwear, were worn for up to a week. Awful! Antiperspirants came in only during my late teens, and I happily took to them.

Papa was a quiet man. I rarely saw him angered. His communication with me was minimal. Not that he did not care, he just did not know how to relate with his son, I think. It was not something done – yet. These were very different times, kids! When he retired at age 65, he was very content to make more money for a few years in retirement than during his final year of employment because of some extra insurance he had taken out. He used to meet regularly with some of his former co-employees, now co-retirees, all of whom seemed to have the highest regard for him. Eventually, his walks with the two Dachshunds they had became less and his strength faded. In the years before his death, when we had supper during my visit, supper consisting usually of a slice of bread or half a bun, he loved to wrap the cold-cut around the bread or bun, biting into it with a mischievous smile.

The year of his death, 1985, five years after my mother had gone, I flew over there three times, whenever he landed in Intensive Care due to his heart giving out. Then, we had planned a vacation with our Morrison friends to travel through southern Germany, Austria and Switzerland, Ute flew in first (at the time Ute and I rarely flew together, so that one would be left, should something happen). She met my father at home, talked with him. I was to come three days later. Papa had died the day Ute saw him. He died of congestive heart failure on September 10, 1985 at age 78. Although he never was a soldier, he followed the adage: "Old soldiers never die, they just fade away".

Except for about two years shortly after The War, mother's brother-in-law, Karl Borth, husband of Marie Borth, née Michels, was unemployed. For a living, it was arranged for them to run the grocery store. This was the only time Mama did not stand in the store until retirement. She had been a tall, good-looking woman. Then, when she entered menopause, better times came to Germany again. The so-called Fresswelle (stuffing wave) began, better and plentiful food became available. Having gone through two periods of nutritional depravation, WW1 and WW2, she got carried away. Her weight increased substantially. This led to various pains and afflictions and heavy medicating. In her later years she became a closet-alcoholic and in physical and, maybe, emotional pain, did not take enough care of herself. She died of a heart attack, collapsing in the middle of preparing food, at age 72 on December 7, 1980.

We never were a prolific family. During the summer of 1943, I was six, my folks induced me to put sugar cubes onto the window sill of my room, this to attract The Stork to bring me a brother or sister. And promptly following this baiting, my sister Hannelore Bärbel was born on September 13, of this year. WW2 had been going on for four years. That year my mother was to be 35 years old and my parents knew that time was running out for having another child – this despite the uncertain times. By the time she was born, things did not look so rosy any more – the tides of war had begun to turn.

Hannelore and I were seven years apart. When she was still a child, I had entered the teens. When I was in my twenties, she was a teenager. Thus we lived our separate lives. She went to a school for commercial training where she became livelong friends with Olli Schmidt. She also began to smoke cigarettes at age 16. My father smoked cigars. He started smoking, when tobacco became scarce, about age 30. During the war and postwar years he grew tobacco in our garden, which he traded for cigars. I never took to the habit.

Upon completion of Hannelore's schooling she eventually took a job with the US military PX system, where she remained, with one interruption, until her death. Again, with only a break of a year, when she lived with us in Canada, she always stayed with my parents. While both of us were insecure children, even as young adults, she never did outgrow this affliction. Only as adults, even only after our father's death, the last of the parents to go, did we find each other. There was only a brief conflict. With the inheritance coming to us, she expected to receive a greater share, claiming that she had stayed, taken care of the parents. While I respected that, I also suggested that she had always had a home, her meals being ready, no expenses to pay, thus had experienced this as a major benefit. As I saw it, the primary reason for her never leaving the parents, was not the care-taking, but rather comfort of home and the fear of self-reliance. I disagreed, and the issue was settled in that she also received one half.

The inheritance from my father, the house on Rheingaustr. 150, which we sold shortly after his death to a long time renter, who had a fast-food joint where the grocery store had been, enabled her to buy a modern condo in Biebrich's center. Getting out of the old house into this modern building was a delight for her. During my visits, maybe only two, we used to sit on the little loggia of her apartment, talking and finding each other. I recall her small delights when, at the end of a day I emptied my pockets of the heavy change one accumulated in Germany, and dropped it into her hands.

Through the years I had gently suggested to quit smoking. Her response was: "When the doctor tells me, I will." Then, when Ute and I had a one day stopover in Singapore, Karen reached us by phone, telling that Hannelore had been diagnosed with lung cancer. My attempts to circumnavigate the globe by flying from Singapore to Frankfurt, instead back to Chicago, were in vain. There was no suitable connection. For her surgery, in which the right lung was removed, I flew to Heidelberg. This I did with my cousin Gerda, our first get-together in, at least, a couple of decades. She, herself, by that time had gone through her own trials and tribulations, having lost her husband to brain cancer, needing to take care of twin boys, then having had a daughter outside marriage. By the time we traveled, her husband Willy Schmidt, had taken them all in and adopted also her daughter! In the

199

consultation with Hannelore's surgeon he told me, that she would have at most two years to live.

We invited her to come to Schaumburg since, unmarried, her friends all working, there was no one to take care of her when it would become necessary. Not that she had accepted that fate at the time. She came and we had a few good weeks, except that she wanted to smoke again! Finally, weakening, and with the kids gone, we set up a hospital bed in the former bedroom of the girls and, together with our friend Judy Morrison, also a nurse, the three of us were able to take care of Hannelore around the clock. Already in Germany, one time not having been careful, she had acquired a bacterial infection in her empty lung cavity, which had to be drained daily from fluids accumulating. This could not be stilled. And, in a repeat with the Indian doctor Karen and I saw on Trinidad – when we contacted a Vietnamese thoracic surgeon to see if anything could be done – he did not charge us, for he could not help!

While Hannelore stayed with us, gradually deteriorating, we arranged for our children to visit to say their good-byes. Olli, Hannelore's friend for twenty years, also came for a couple of weeks. Also never married, with only a long-term relationship with her married boss, which I had several years earlier urged her to quit, she had lost in Hannelore her main support in life. Already before she had taken to drinking, went through several withdrawal cures which, however, never took hold. It must have been within a year of Hannelore's death that we received notice that she had taken her life.

Hannelore, having been a good-looking woman, yet never able to 'catch' a mate, faded away and in Ute's presence died much too early at age 47 on January 26, 1991. We returned her ashes to Germany for a final ceremony with relatives and friends. She and my parents were interned at the cemetery in Biebrich, their little vaults rented for 25 years. Thus, when I went there in May of 2004, my mother's remains had already been removed and spread in a common area of the cemetery.

3. My Birth and Younger Years

On May 5th, 1934 my parents had tied the knot and on Sept. 29, 1936 I came along. We lived in this old house on Elisabethenstraße 1, the oldest neighborhood in Wiesbaden's suburb of Biebrich, I later called "a scrubby little industrial town" of about 30,000. Our neighborhood wasn't very rarified – to say the least. But my folks always considered themselves a cut above their surroundings and kept conveying that to me – particularly my paternal grandmother who lived with us! It must have contributed to my feeling to be an elitist (of whatever qualification), yet always having had also a down-to-earth appreciation of and respect for 'common' folks. When my parents married they put running water and electricity into the house they rented. At least, I think they rented it. Two sides of the building were covered entirely by a vine, which gave it a homey feeling. The small yard could be closed off by a heavy gate. In late childhood, I used to collect dead little birds in the neighborhood to bury them alongside a wall in the yard.

As I said before, my mother helped her mother run the grocery store. I do not recall from when-on, but I seem to have been left rather early in the care of my paternal grandmother, Omi, as she was called. My mother's mother was Oma. Recall, that I called Omi a strong-willed woman. And I recall in only one event – I do not know what my age was at the time – that I was made to go back and shut the door to our living room properly. She loved, what she called "Dämmerstündchen", the little dusk hour when, in the wintertime she sat in an old, worn easy chair, I on what was left of her lap, and told me fairy tales of which she knew many. I grew up on fairy tales. I think they were very real to me to the extent, that I came to imagine having a brother in Holland, although this fellow did not play any major role in my mind. Yet, much later, I conjectured, that these engrossing fairy tales impacted my growing up substantially – to the negative.

A major content of fairy tales is, that almost anything is magically possible. Way into my adulthood – and I certainly learned that it wasn't so – my mindset was geared to thinking, that anything coming up to challenge me I could tackle without preparation, whether this required mental or physical strength. Not that I believed in magic!

Across from my maternal grandmother's house on Rheingaustraße 150, Elisabethenstraße was in between, stood a tall apartment building. Family friends, the Klages, lived there on the third floor. Uncle Karl had a son in his twenties who was serving in the Luftwaffe. He was a pilot. On one of his visits he grabbed me by my clothing and body, I was maybe four years old, and held me, kicking and screaming, over the balcony of the apartment. I attribute my acrophobia to this terrifying experience. What all was not done at the time to toughen kids up for the Führer!

Just beyond, a block from my maternal grandmother's house, all about 60 meters from the banks of the river Rhine, stood a large chateau, behind which extended a substantial park. I recall my father taking me there for Sunday walks, also along the river. During my teens I used to walk the many pathways of this park. On one in particular, thick bushes left and right, one could hear the song of nightingales in spring and inhale the wafting scents of Jasmine. On another trail fireflies galore cavorted in the bushes at dusk. Not too many years later, none could be seen any more, probably due to the application of insecticides and other ecological deterioration.

Together with a large vegetable garden located about half a kilometer from the homes beyond the chateau grounds, these locales introduced me to nature. My father had planted many fruit trees, some were already older. There were berries and all kinds of vegetables. I also had to help out there hand-watering the produce. This water had to be hand-pumped from a well. When the old well had partially collapsed, it had to be renewed. For that my father had delivered several sections of concrete rings about one meter in diameter by half a meter in height. The first ring was put level above the well. Then the ground below and around it was dug out for it to sink lower. When its upper face became level with the ground, the next section was put on top and the digging process continued. Eventually, with me being smaller and more flexible, I had the exclusive task down in the well and water to complete the digging.

In the earlier years the hand pump poured the water into a large zinc bathtub from where it had to be carried by watering cans all across the rather large garden of probably 3/5 of an acre. Then my dad

202

put in three big steel barrels, at correspondingly lower levels, connected by a small diameter pipe system. Now one could pump water into the first barrel, from which it flowed to the other two, greatly facilitating watering. And I got permission to cart the big zinc tub to the metal recycler and got to keep the proceeds.

Aside from an old barn on the garden's property in which rabbits were raised during the war and postwar years which, I recall, were stolen at one time, there was a ramshackle little hut, its front open. A small old table and some chairs sometimes served for a Sunday afternoon picnic – after some gardening, of course.

I recall to have climbed a mirabelle tree one late afternoon, no one else being with me. I had propped up several boards of different length to climb up to the first crook when, during the ascent, they collapsed. Being practical, I first had my fill. But then I had to get down. It looked awfully high from up top. I sat and sat, not daring to jump. Dusk came and I had to make a decision!

Once, in later years, father and I had taken down the dried-up pole beans and piled them up for burning. Dad poured some gasoline over it for better ignition. Then he threw a match on the heap and, whoosh, it ignited wonderfully, so much so, that the two of us, looking sheepishly at each other, did so with singed eyebrows and front hair.

Another impressive experience took place in 1942 and 43 when first my parents and I traveled for a vacation to Bavaria. The mountains, their evening glow in the sun, the beautiful lakes left a deep impression on me, which would have been even better, had I not suffered from wind pox and worms. In 1943 Omi, my father, a family friend, Karl Klages, and I went to the same place. There was a small floating dock at the Barmsee, by which the hotel was located. We used to sit on a small bench on the dock. Uncle Karl employed a sieve with a long handle attached to catch crayfish, small fish and snails in the weeds below the dock. When I returned to this place in 1952, the waters were sterile. Not a single creature could I see. There was talk, that an American bomber had crashed into the lake towards the end of the war. Was that it? I also recall the first erotic stirrings there at the tender age of six at the nearby swimming lake, the Grubsee, when the slipping top of a pubescent girl revealed a budding breast.

When I was about five years old, some time in 1941, I was operated in Wiesbaden for an inguinal hernia I had acquired at age one, supposedly from a very hard laugh. Only very much later did I learn, that males are frequently afflicted by such hernias, due to the descent of the testes into the scrotum, weakening the groin muscles. I had been wearing a hernia harness for all these years. And it so happened, that in a night after the surgery an air raid alarm was given. I have the dim memory of patients' beds being moved from their rooms to inside hallways of the hospital. It was impossible to get patients to a shelter. This was one of the few times that a localized bombing of Wiesbaden took place.

Not much later bombing raids became frequent. First the nighttime raids by the British, later daytime raids by the Americans. By that time I was seven, and the nightly air raid advance warnings literally scared the shit out of me. All too often one of my folks had to first clean me up in the bathtub before we could take to a nearby shelter. Our house did not have a basement. Although our neighborhood never experienced direct bomb impacts, I was deathly afraid of the heavy thuds of explosions happening within kilometers. At least twice my father had to grab me by the seat of my pants to pull me down the shelter's stairs when I rushed off to get outside, into the open, unaware that it was much more dangerous there. After a raid, I recall, he took me to the roof of the tall apartment building that housed the shelter to show me the sea of flames that had been the city of Mainz! There was also the interminable stretching of time I experienced, caused by the tick-tock of the grandfather clock in our living room between advance warnings and the actual warning or when things remained up in the air and we had to wait some time before being able to go to bed again. After one raid I was told later by my parents, that several incendiary bombs had struck Oma's house, most of them being duds. But in some the phosphorous had started smoldering and all had to be extracted and removed by my folks by, I do not know, what means.

Thus, in late summer of 1944 my father brought me by train and some walking to family friends in Jagsthausen in the country, where I would not be exposed to the increasing air raids. The only "remote" experience of a bombing raid I experienced in Jagsthausen was when Heilbronn, a city about 20 km distant was attacked. With no shelters in the village, its people walked out of the settlement into the surrounding fields.

Years later, living already in the US, when my mother sent me my childhood drawings, I found that practically all were depictions of air raids! And for many years later, way into my adulthood, when I heard the sound of multi-propeller planes in the night, I was instantly awake and alert. Mind you, by that time I didn't poop into my pajamas any more. The advent of jet planes with their different engine noise freed me from these memories.

Jagsthausen was a haven for me. I could explore the countryside with my peers, smoke corn silk and other implements and just get into miscellaneous other kinds of minor troubles, particularly after school, which took place in a single classroom for all grades. During the war's final months schooling had been suspended. Before that happened, or maybe even afterwards, we tikes were at times delegated to pick potato beetles and to thin out and properly space sugar beet sprouts. I recall taking off at one time with some fellow-conspirators from potato beetle collection, which we didn't care for, since it gave us yucky fingers from the beetles' excretions. To get home we forded the small Jagst river and I recall the strong current we had to fight.

The family friend I stayed with, who had lost her husband in Russia, had a son, a bit younger than I, who snored. With the two of us sleeping in one bed, I was annoyed by this snoring and pinched him to make him stop. This he told his mother, so that an unused storage room was fixed up for me to sleep in. The 2000-soul village had a small church, not far from where we lived, with a clock that chimed the time every quarter hour. Right after my "internment" in this room I recall creatures running across my bed in the night, bumps sounding from somewhere, and the clock chiming midnight – the witching hour. Was I scared! Then I suffered through the following hour. A mouse hunt got under way the next day, and the bumps turned out to be the next door farmer's pigs bumping their stall. But what did this matter to a just seven year old. One time I got to ring the church bell and recall how the rope pulled me off my feet into the air, once I got it going.

But I could also build small dams and waterwheels in rivulets in the woods. In the winter of 44/45 jump a horse-drawn snow plow that went to some outlying farms without telling anyone and getting back frozen stiff at nighttime. Playing on an open slope outside the village when a very low-flying fighter aircraft approached us straight on, with us waving to it wildly, thinking it to be German, when it turned out to be American. Had its pilot opened fire... From there we also threw rocks down onto the road trying to explode BB shells.

I believe my parents visited Jagsthausen twice while I lived there – by bicycle! This meant dodging various obstacles on the way, among which were Allied fighters planes on the hunt. Not that two bicyclists would have made much of a target, but one never knew. If my memory is correct, my father, on one of these trips carried U-boat hull plans – no weirs were built during the war, everything and everyone was dedicated to the war machinery – to Augsburg, where another M.A.N. plant was located – by bicycle! What a way to lose a war!

When things really turned ugly the beginning of 1945, my father had organized a truck from his employer and brought more family members from Biebrich to Jagsthausen. Here's a story told so often by my folks, that it became one of my own "as if" experiences. On their truck journey from Biebrich to Jagsthausen the travelers were at one time directed by German soldiers to take cover because of an imminent air raid. Everyone hopped or slid off the truck to find whatever cover was to be had. When "Entwarnung", all clear, was given my paternal grandmother, the fire-spitting dragon as I called her years after her death, was nowhere to be found. Eventually some muffled sounds were heard. And the rather corpulent woman was found stuck in a culvert she had dashed in headlong, but was now unable to extract herself from. The hilariousness of being stuck, needing to be pulled out by her feet, must have broken the tension of the attack, at least for the others not having been so confined.

Then, in May, a small contingent of German troops entered the village "to defend" it. The mayor was able to convince them, that it wasn't worth it and – lo – they went on, but only after blowing up one span of the centuries-old beautiful stone bridge spanning the Jagst – when a really shallow ford lay just downstream from it!

Then American tanks entered – and I got to know my first chewing gum. The Yanks set up shower facilities by the river and we boys were at times invited to also clean up in there. We, certainly, could use it, and it was the first time I got to see nude men. Dressed, I also watched them fishing in the Jagst with hand grenades. Then, when things had settled down a bit, my dad got that truck again which, by the way was powered by a "Holzvergaser", a power system using wood gas generated by on-board wood-chips, and took us all back to Biebrich. Before that happened, Uncle Karl, mother's brother-in-law had returned from his imprisonment as a P.O.W. He smoked, but nothing was available, except the butts of American soldiers. He asked us to collect same for him. One day I found half a cigar a Yank had discarded. Instead of turning it in to Uncle Karl, I smoked it, or some of it, and got violently ill. It may have been this experience, which saved me from ever taking up smoking. For some years later, I just dabbled a bit in it here and there.

As is apparent from the above, my father did not have to serve in the military. He had become a minor Nazi official, but the main reason seems to have been his experience as an engineer in river weir design. In that context he was twice required to travel to Russia during the German advance to assist in the repair of the giant hydroelectric dam at Dnjepopetrovsk in Ukraine. In the postwar years, after de-Nazification, he became the chief engineer in the M.A.N.s weir design and building department. He might have become its director, but that would have required a doctorate or at least a masters. His' was only the equivalent of a BS, its owner in Germany called in jest, a "narrow gage" engineer.

4. To the Teen-Years

In the fall of 1945 grammar schooling resumed. In the fall of 1946 I had become ten and it was time to get into "higher" schooling, customary and as desired by my parents.

Before I can elaborate on my unsuccessful schooling experience, I must tell of another venture of the times. Before and during the war produce for the grocery store had been delivered by farmers from across the Rhine River in the state of Rhineland Palatinate. The left bank of the Rhine was now under French occupation. We lived on the right bank, in the American sector. We had the better deal, also access to little goodies, like sewing needles, etc. It wasn't that easy for adults to get across the makeshift bridge to Mainz and beyond. I did, with a backpack and little trade goods, which I bartered with the previous store suppliers for produce. I also paid for such. Once, when I had taken a year younger neighbor's boy along, we were asked by a stranger in the tram how we had acquired the produce. He answered: "We begged for them". I was totally disgusted. I had been a trader, not a beggar. I believe it was the only time he came along! See, my "commercial" roots go back a long way.

Every once in a while the Rhine River used to flood in spring, which inundated the cellar in the house on Rheingaustraße 150, also frequently required the installation of raised boardwalks alongside the houses. The postwar years were particularly hard for many people, not that I at age ten, had much awareness of this. Even the occasional corpse that was fished out of the river, did not leave much of an impression. What was death at that age! The waters were polluted. There were no purification plants on line at that time. Feces and other garbage floated downstream and the water stank from hydrocarbons and other refuse. Still, people fished in there, like my 'Uncle Klages' to supplement the meager provisions. I recall the three segments of a skinned and gutted eel still twitching in their frying pan. At another time my mother refused to ever again clean and prepare a batch of freshly caught Rhine-fish because of their odor.

I also grew up with fairy tale stories of another kind such as, that masturbation led to softening of the spine. Many years later it led to the resolve not to carry this baggage along. And, although, it produced an opening up, it was also too much for the children. There were also other fears, causing me to have a 10" spike beside my bed for protection against whatever might come in the dark or have been hiding under my bed, even though I always checked that before retiring.

Back to school. I recall we were 61 pupils in the Sexta, as the first class in the Realgymnasium was called. Looking back, I sure wasn't ready for higher learning! Diversions were many. Some were sexual explorations during school hours, the reading of little stories written by a class mate, or just dreaming. I wasn't with it. The imaginary world held sway. Having begun to read adventure stories did not help either. I muddled through to the next higher class, the Quinta. English was a required subject from the Sexta's beginning. Then I moved up to the Quarta, where Latin was introduced. I recall that teachers had moved me right up front to the first row. It wasn't much use. My grades fell all into the D and F range. But I loved to draw maps of other countries in Erdkunde, the study of the world, yet still produced a D.

Once, when I managed to write a C- in an English test, my teacher, by the name of Schuhmacher, the only teacher's name I still recall, told me: "Even a blind chicken finds a piece of grain once in a while". Very assuring and helpful! Could I only once talk to Herr Schuhmacher these days. Well, I had to do the Quarta again! When we failed tests so-called Blue Letters were mailed to our parents to inform them of the failings of their offspring. I was deathly afraid of them, but not enough. In order to help me perform better in tests, I used to pray 20-plus Lord's prayers before having to write such tests – it never worked! But study I did not. This seems to have been a major contributing factor in my loss of faith – if ever there really existed one. Do not take me too seriously on this!

Here and there I played a little soccer, nothing to brag about, just kicking a ball around. In school we had sports. When we received our grades in the fall, I was always the best in summer sports, the hundred meter dash, the broad and the high jump. When spring grades came, I was the last in line. Indoor sports, climbing poles, ropes, or exercises on the horse were not for me. Upper body strength was missing. I just never was an athlete.

We had also music lessons at school. Now, remember the tobacco dad grew in our garden. When it was dried in the loft of the old barn, it left a crumbly tobacco powder on the newspaper. Having found out, that this powder was very conducive to produce heavy sneezing when inhaled, I took some a couple of times to music lessons and blew it covertly, of course, around me. It produced satisfying results! Then I must have been stupid enough to admit to it, or even boast about it. In any case, the music teacher found out and I was called to a separate room, was made to bend over a chair, and got a good whopping with a cane. Is that, why I have never been good at music? Sure, I learned to enjoy it, particularly Bach and Beethoven, in later years, but I have no comprehension of its esoterics. Too bad!

My father was an atheist or agnostic, I do not know which; my mother a ho-hum Christian. In grammar school I had been excused from religious studies, but later was sent to instructions for confirmation.

Well, and after I had done the Quarta twice and failed it that second time, I was expelled. What was my poor father and mother to do with this failure? Had they not hoped I could become an engineer, a doctor, or whatever, moving up the social ladder? Had Omi not exhorted me to study or, if not, I would have to go with a little lunch pail to the Knochenmühle, the stinking factory a kilometer down the road, where they made glue and gelatin from bones. What was left for me to do, to learn? So Papa stuck me into an apprenticeship as an industrial maintenance mechanic at the large company he worked about 7 km away. The M.A.N., as it was called, trained about 200 apprentices at this facility. Now I was in a blue-collar environment, was teased by my fellow apprentices about my 'midwife's hands' – and thoroughly learned to dislike it. I was now 14 years old.

However, apprentices were paid, about 70 marks a month. From my savings I soon bought a good 35 mm camera, a Kodak

Retina. I used it for many years, until I found, that I saw the world too much through a viewfinder. Thus I stopped, deciding that I'd rather forget what I had seen, but to see it, to live it, right then in the present. Soon, it also turned out that I was quite good at technical drawing. And so, two years into my three year apprenticeship I was pulled out of the shop environment to produce technical drawings required by the director for apprentices, a friend of my father's. I spent my last year in a little room adjacent to his office improving my drawing abilities. During these years I started to read voraciously, much in areas of popular science, etc. I improved my education. While in the shop I associated more with older boys, who had already a 10-12 year education and served a practicum of only 1-2 years. With them I devised games testing one's knowledge about various subjects. So, when the time came for testing to acquire my journeyman's certificate I finished in the top four of 50 finishers. I had left my "fantasy world" behind and faced reality! Following this, I was offered employment as a draftsman in one of the company's engineering departments for large irrigation and cooling pumps. Now I had a monthly income of several hundred marks. As it evolved, I think I can safely say, that I was the best technical draftsman I've ever come across.

I had developed a certain wittiness, was able to make little puns. This newfound ability I used on my dad in a non-threatening way. It often elicited a smile. When I saw that smile I knew I had made contact. But this was about the best contact I was able to make. While my father was not a stern or uncaring man, he was remote. This I explained to myself by him not having grown up with a father, not having learned how to interact with his son. And there were no "outside" lessons, such as swimming, music, sports, or whatever. None!

Not having known any grandfather, both had died before I was born, I grew up in a women-dominated family. Both, my grandmothers and my mother were strong women. But this I understood only many years, decades later. I think it also caused me later to be comfortable with strong women.

5. Growing up

But the experience of failure at the Realgymnasium had left a mental scar. I was insecure and timid. From age 14 to 20 I had no close friends. At 15 my parents and I vacationed at Lake Konstanz (Lac Lemans). At 16 I made my first solo-excursion by bus to Bavaria to revisit the area near Mittenwald, where we had stayed in 42/43. At trip down memory lane. And I kept reading.

In the summer of 1951 at a swimming facility on the adjacent Rhine island, I learned swimming. Even then the waters were still not very kosher. No one these days would immerse himself into such a 'broth'. A couple of years later I got my certificate as an accomplished swimmer – which I never really was – by swimming three kilometers downstream – in that broth! But better things happened at this swimming facility. I had my first crush on a girl from the neighborhood, Hilde Backhaus, which led nowhere. But in that same year, at age 15, I came across this svelte blonde, schoolmate and best friend of my cousin Gerda. With that, we now enter into my extended family. My mother's brother, Fritz Jakob Michels, had become chief electrical engineer at Dyckerhoff Cement Works in Amöneburg, a town located a couple of kilometers from Biebrich. He and his wife had a nice, spacious apartment and four children, three of which were in my age group. Fritz, the oldest, namesake of his father, was two years older than I. Liesel, a year older, Gerda was my age, and a late comer, Christa, several years younger. Gerda and I were the "intellectual" ones, without us knowing it at that time, and were here and there gravitating toward each other. Just as my parents met with uncle Fritz's family, I often walked the two km to play with my cousins and other neighborhood kids.

That play consisted of hopping through the railroad cars parked on the ramp leading to the blown-up railroad bridge that once crossed the Rhine here. Flying kites from that ramp, opening the big shells of antiaircraft guns that had been positioned near the bridge, putting the powder on the tram tracks that passed by there to "scare" the drivers and passengers. Putting, what we called carbide powder in discarded bottles, then throwing them in the Rhine where entering water developed a gas, causing the bottles to explode. All of us were lucky. No one ever got hurt.

I must have been 16 when I joined the Biebrich Rowing Club. If there was ever a sport I enjoyed, it was this. While I never rowed or sculled competitively (a rower uses one oar, a sculler two somewhat smaller ones), it was fun on the water, excellent whole-body exercise and good company with fellow-rowers. There were even a couple of overnight rowing trips. At that time I used to carry my hair long, which became a nuisance while rowing. That's when I cut it short to a brush-cut, similar to the one my father had worn for most of his life.

At 16 I also went for dancing lessons in Wiesbaden, incidentally meeting there Ute's (Ute, the svelte blonde) older sister Christa. And so, weekend sing-alongs and dances evolved to take place at my uncle's residence. The sing-alongs usually turned me off, or rather not on, and I felt left out. In any case, at that time my feeling was, that my extended family, including my immediate one, was much too emotional. I wanted to separate myself from this felt emotionality. Little did I know, and only much later discovered, that I was never able to distance myself from deeply felt emotional subjects.

But dancing I enjoyed, within limits. I loved to dance the Tango in particular with Ute. But again and again – I was timid. At the time, Ute called me "the living corpse". An attempt to invite her to a movie got me her father on the phone. And as it happened, she had a cold at the time, and her father wasn't about to let her go with that unknown caller. And that was it.

Being friends with Gerda, Ute gravitated more to my uncle's family, especially after her parents went back to Indonesia in the mid-fifties. Without her own family, my uncle's became the substitute. And thus she latched on to my cousin, Fritz, with me looking on from afar. When, at one time – she had already moved away to become a dietitian assistant – she cooked an Indonesian Ricetafel at my uncle's home, I was smitten by the taste experience...

During these years I resolved to improve my English and took evening classes. There I became acquainted with twins, brother and sister, a bit younger than I, both quite educated, the parents seemingly rather well off. These kids were avowed communists and in the few meetings I had with them and others in their group, we got into some heated discussions. Remember – me being The Capitalist!

When I was 17, an age-mate neighbor of our group, Herbert Carl, mentioned the plans of an older friend of his to travel to Sweden where this fellow had worked for a year. And as these things evolve, a group of four came together, two older ones with driver's licenses, and the two Herbert's, too young to have one already. Off we went in a VW beetle, of course. Up at big Lake Vänern on the camping place where we stayed near Karlstad, the other guys (me too) met a couple of Swedish girls. It was midsummer time, and the other Herbert fell for one of them. Towards the end of our stay in Sweden, on a camping place near Malmo, while the other three played Skat in our tent, a German card game, I walked a short distance to a small jetty extending west into the sea. A stela of unknown purpose provided an eerie backdrop. At the tip of the jetty I stood, alone, facing the setting sun, and sang into the wind and the falling dusk, falling into a trance. Then it happened – I felt I had become one with the world and the world had become one with me. It was the most profound spiritual experience I've ever had.

Rudyard Kipling, speaking through one of his important characters, the Lama Teshoo, towards the end of his novel 'Kim', expressed a similar profound experience:

'Yea, my Soul went free, wheeling like an eagle, saw indeed that there was no Teshoo Lama nor any other Soul. As a drop draws to water, so my Soul drew near to the Great Spirit which is beyond all things. At that point, exalted in contemplation, I saw all Hind, from Ceylon in the sea to the Hills, and my own Painted Rock at Suchzen; I saw every camp and village, to the least, where we have ever rested. I saw them at one time and in one place; for they were within the Soul. By this I knew the Soul had passed beyond the illusion of Time and Space and Things. By this I knew that I was free...'

So, next year, Herbert and I had by then acquired our driver licenses, my father relinquished his VW beetle for a couple of weeks and we drove up to Sweden once again. During my teens, I was very much taken by jazz and used to hum and improvise while driving. I did this also on a cross-country drive from Karlstad to Uddevalla to visit relatives of our Swedish friends and was promptly asked to "perform" for them that evening – which I promptly declined to do. On the spur of the moment I invited Birgitta Forsen's (Herbert's crush) younger brother, maybe 11 years old, to come back with us to Germany for a visit. This his parents allowed. Subsequently we shipped him back by train. Next year, 1956, Herbert Carl moved to Sweden. But Birgitta, with a 146 IQ was apparently too much for him. They parted. But Herbert found another love and remained in Sweden. For several years a tenuous contact was maintained via my parents, when he visited Germany – alas – eventually that ended. Once, on a visit to Chicago, he tried to find us in the Chicago phone book, but did not search the many suburban phone directories. So, to my regret, we never met again. My later searches on the internet were in vain.

I must have been around 18 when the question: What do I live for? came to a head. While I had be "confirmed" at age 14, I had distanced myself more and more from "Christian teachings". One evening, walking home in Wiesbaden, I arrived at my profound definition: To live and to make the best of it! Shortly thereafter, the question arose: Sure, but by what rule? And I decided: To protect and further life, but when necessary also to terminate it. I have done the latter, but in some respects failed at the former. It must not have been much later, that I officially declared my exit from the Lutheran Church. A minor issue was that, in Germany, 10% of one's federal taxes are deducted and transferred to the church to which one belongs.

One more down-to-Earth thing. The house on Rheingaustr. 150 had three floors. We occupied the ground floor and the first. There were two entrances, one up front and one on the side, the one on the side leading up to an entrance to dad's study. Once, when I opened the front door, a pair of Jehovah's Witnesses attempted to convert me. I was able to discourage them, but before they left, they asked, whether the gentleman up on the first floor was my father. Afterwards inquired with Papa how he dealt with these people. He put on his mischievous grin and said: "I just stand there". Well, is asked: "How does that get them to give up?" Well, he answered: "What's there to talk about, if they get no response."

6. Change is in the Air

I was itchy approaching 20. I had seen a little bit of the world. And I had read even more. I entertained thoughts of bicycling around the world, stories I had read about. To that my parents said: No.

Then I hit on the idea of traveling by motor bike through Africa. By that time they figured they had to let me go somehow, so I got their heavy-hearted blessing and cooperation. I was still not of legal age! But a companion had to be found. This I did in the person of a fellow-apprentice I had remained in contact with. He became my junior partner. I had saved and saved, even from my desk at the office had sold all kinds of "stuff", cigarettes, candy, even liquor to my colleagues at work just to make an extra buck. Then I bought a DKW motorcycle and subsequently attached a side car. The sidecar's opening was fitted with a solid, lockable steel lid. The whole rig was underpowered.

The comments I got from people, particularly my uncle Fritz, were something like: I was going to make babies with millet bellies in Africa. It all was a rather uncommon enterprise for the people I knew. And then, on October 1, 1956 – I obviously had quit my job as a draftsman – and a week after I had two infected molars pulled, we took off.

After a stop at the DKW factory for a minor overhaul we crossed the Alps, freezing assorted appendages off, until we exited a tunnel arriving at the Mediterranean. All down the Italian boot it went to Naples, where we boarded a steamer to take us to Tripoli in Libya where, at the time, King Idris still ruled. Colonel Gadhafi was yet to come. On board we met three other Germans, the older one married to a French woman, the two younger ones a bit older than us 20 year olds. They traveled in a little Fiat car, intent on a similar route through Africa. We resolved to travel together, at least for a time. Out of Tripoli date palm groves stretched for many kilometers. We did not make it beyond them that day and had to camp beside the road. Here and there people lived in little huts below the palm trees. We decided to post guards in one and on half hour rotations, excluding the woman. When my stint came the previous guy told me: "There's an old man coughing over there. And when you hear 'plops' from time to time, that's just dates dropping from the trees." Well, he was the one with diaharrea all the way to Kairo, having eaten these misbegotten dates in the dark, either not fully ripened or somehow rotten.

At Benghazi we were stopped by some Germans, employed at the local British air base, and invited to stay there overnight. These fellows were leftovers from the war, had stayed on after having been released as POWs, and now had their own facilities, even a bar, where I got to know my first Scotch – warm and as a shot. I had a bad night sleeping on an exercise mat in their gym. Usually, we slept in our two-man tent – without air mattresses! (Upon my return to Germany the tent bottom looked like a sieve having slept all too often on rocky ground) We didn't like the Arab flatbread and were happy to find white bread, introduced when Libya was an Italian colony. We bought tiny chicken eggs from children on the outskirts of a miserable little village, which turned out to be cooked for preservation. No scrambled eggs that night. And we watched dung beetles rolling away our discard for their offspring. The acres of white crosses at El Alamein left a deep impression. In October/November it rains in North Africa. Often we got soaked in the morning, then scorched in the afternoon, particularly once we had entered Egypt, where the coast drops somewhat southward.

We entered Kairo and found, lo and behold, cheap lodging at a place run by protestant sisters. We saw some of the local sights, met new people, some at our place of stay, some outside. We were dinner guests of a Jewish couple – yes, there were still some Jews in Kairo at the time, but then the sky fell. Nasser had nationalized the Suez Canal several weeks before, something the French and British owners of the facilities did not appreciate. So, together with the Israelis, they attacked Egypt, largely by air, until US President Eisenhower put a stop to it. But the moment the attack started we could no longer leave the house, since a mob would have quickly gathered, thinking us to be downed enemy flyers. For two weeks we were stuck at our lodging – and don't think it was fancy – watching the air attacks on outlying facilities from the roof of our house. At times we fried some eggs on our camp stove together with pastorma, a lean paprika and pepper-coated beef, to vary our diet. The eggshells and some other refuse went out the window. We lived the way like many locals did. The forced stay reduced our cash, though. For three days I encountered my first, what in Egypt one would have to call Pharao's decease. Debilitating! Upon recovery an about 50 year old German nurse, bicycling from Berlin to Nairobi – at least, that was her intent – she had come via Spain all along the North African coast, offered to darn my socks. A 30 year old more worldly Austrian I had befriended at the place cautioned me: She ain't after your socks!

Finally, we were able to go onto the streets again, but still, twice were we stopped by a mob, shouting Anglesi, Francaui, penning us in. Usually a bespectacled English-speaking man in the crowd took us to the next police station. After identification, the Austrian fellow had it made with the station commander who knew that Hitler had been Austrian. We were never physically assaulted. One day, my Austrian friend, who had lived in various North African countries and spoke fluent Arabic, invited me to visit that evening with a couple of Egyptian women. It was a proper social setting, nevertheless for the times unusual. The older one, in her early thirties, was married to a German who, at the time, was stuck in Germany, since all flights had been suspended. The younger cousin of hers, about my age, had just been divorced by her Egyptian husband. My lasting impression of that evening was of how both women tore into the repressive fabric of their Islamic culture.

By that time virtually all foreigners had been evacuated from Egypt, mostly by river boat up the Nile into Khartoum, Sudan, to fly out from there. Mostly only hard-core "adventurers" were left. The 50 year old nurse left to bicycle south to Aswan, about 700 km, only to return since the Sudanese immigration officer in Aswan would stamp her passport only after 6 PM at his home. Yes, various other interesting characters did we meet en route. Then we heard, that Egyptian banks were accepting English pound traveler checks again. Without verifying this, I and my companion, Gernot Winkler, thought it time to head south. We had one of the lodge employees paint Alemani, German, in large yellow Arabic letters on the lid of our side car – at least we hoped that it was what it said, and took off. Our advice had been not to camp anywhere along the Nile or in the desert, but to check in at a police station. This we did the first night and were asked to wait. At 6 PM we were told to follow two officers, were taken to an old guest house dating from British colonial times, a mansion by any standard. There we were treated by the two gentlemen to a sumptuous dinner where, for the first time I got to taste pomegranates. I was not impressed by the itty-bitty kernels. The night was spent in a soft bed with lots of mosquitos attacking us through the open windows. On it went the next day over dusty roads to another stay at a police station and a friendly reception.

Then we entered Luxor, saw Karnak and Rameses buildings, crossed the Nile with a guide to see the Valley of the Kings, the Colossi of Memnon, and the Temple of Queen Hatchepsut – without a single other tourist ever in sight. This is the place, where in the mid 1990s about 60 tourists were machine-gunned by Islamic terrorists. When I heard about it, I was back at the wide open expanse in front of Hatchepsut's temple, which did not offer any place to hide. I recall my ride on a donkey to get to these locales as one of the most painful experiences to my spine, due to the ass's staccato steps. When we returned to the other bank of the Nile our cash was all gone and the lack of a tip made our guide furious. On it went to Aswan. We had thought to be able to cash some of our traveler checks there, however, it turned out that this was still not possible. So we went to see "the" Sudanese immigration officer. We had Sudanese visas and hoped to drive through the desert into the Sudan, maybe 30-40 kilometers south, where we would be liquid again. The galabeia-clad man walked out of his office, looked at our bike – and shook his head. No go! Stuck – with no money.

We drove up and down Aswan's main street, not knowing what to do. Then we saw a Mercedes with a German license plate. In a small, dirty hotel room we found its owner – with two young women – on their attempted way to Kenia without having a Sudanese visa. I told of our predicament, while all the while I felt quite uncomfortable in this room. And when the guy suggested, that he knew a merchant in a side street where it would be easy to "acquire" some money towards evening, we quickly retreated.

On the street again. And then, unbelievingly, I saw the sign of a protestant mission. Up we drove and in we went to speak to the missionary, who must have heard many a story. But I showed him my here worthless traveler checks, which assuaged him. When I happened to tell him that my godmother was a protestant sister running an orphanage in Germany, I had crept up another notch. He even knew the place. Then I offered my light meter as security and received ten Egyptian pounds, I believe. A year later the lightmeter was returned to me by my godmother, Tante Ina, as I called her, who had vacationed on one of the German North Sea isles, where she met another sister vacationing from Egypt, who had brought my lightmeter along . Small world! Liquid once more we were, but only enough for gas and food to get back to Kairo. We drove out of Aswan and, maybe 30 km north and off the dirt road, set up camp in the desert. It was early in the evening and sleep did not come. Finally, we decided to break camp – and drove through the night and the other day straight back to Kairo, where we re-met some of our other fellow-sufferers. At least we had not been asked to come for the visa stamp at six to "the" immigration officer's home.

What to do now? We heard of the Hungarian uprising being in full swing. Entering the Sudan we could not. To pay for transportation through parts of the Sudan would have seriously depleted our meager funds and, finally, my companion and I didn't really get along well. A colleague of my father's was stationed at the M.A.N.'s representation in Kairo. From him I was able to obtain a loan. The Austrian fellow was eager to get back home. My companion wanted to stay on. So I paid him off; he had been the junior partner anyway, and my new companion and I went on our way home. One night, camping in the desert, we heard a distant voice and bells ringing, all sounding like a shepherd with his flock. Figuring that it was what we thought we, nevertheless, slept only lightly. The next morning, we were just preparing breakfast, the shepherd, a Bedouin, showed up at our tent. My friend could converse with him in Arabic and invited him for breakfast. We had black tea, scrambled eggs and fried pastorma. It was interesting to observe that our visitor partook only of the tea and the eggs, but not the pastorma (it could have been pork, which it wasn't), and only after my friend had first tasted each.

The bike was slowly but surely loosing its integrity – maybe that Sudanese fellow saved my life! We rode to Benghazi, with a few adventures on the way. There we picked a ship to take us over to Sicily and headed straight into a continuous swell and I got quite queazy, also from the complete little octopus that was served us for lunch one day, together with some boiled potatoes and a few leaves of lettuce. The worldly Austrian ate mine too.

In mountainous southern Italy my companion, who didn't have a cycle license and had to ride on the back seat, had to walk quite a few hills, since the bike wouldn't carry the two of us any longer. So we took a train to Rome, where I had the cycle repaired. Before that a small mishap happened to him. We had lost the muffler and, entering the city, he had to put his right shoe over the exhaust as a makeshift sound suppressor – we didn't want to get into an Italian jail. When he stepped off the bike, he collapsed. His plastic shoe heel had melted away. Soon we left the Eternal City again to drive north. Towards the Swiss border it got too cold. It was now close to Christmas. We booked ourselves into a train at Chiasso. The only other fellow-traveller in our compartment was an Israeli medical officer. Talking about our experiences and wonderment that we had never seen a single Egyptian fighter interceptor during the hostilities, he explained: "Oh, Egyptian pilots are excellent flyers and top gunners. But they cant' do both together". Our splurge to the dining car, I was almost home and did no longer need to turn a penny around, had me appreciate and love Gorgonzola cheese for the first time and forever after. Somewhere on this train ride my Austrian companion parted to get home and I never heard from him again. The long uphill walks in Italy may have set him against me. And then I made my mother a wonderful Christmas present when I stood the morning of the 24th in front of the door.

Yet the greatest gift I had given myself – by having done what I did.

7. Opening Up

Home again. I didn't make it to East Africa and down to Cape Town as had been the intention. I needed a job and went back to my old one. But something had changed. Few people at the time had done something like this. The postwar years had not been conducive to such ventures, and prewar adventurers were now older or had perished in the war. I had become "interesting" to others by being able to talk a good story. Oh, by the way, as I then found out, my former companion, Gernot, had made it to Addis Ababa in Ethiopia after all – with the 50 year old nurse.

A young man about two or three years older than I used to purchase his victuals at my mother's grocery store. Already, while I was still on my trip, he had expressed interest in meeting me on my return. And so we did. Wilfried Wolf, at first, writing this, I could not recall his full name, was way ahead of me. He had one serious failing, in that he used high-valutin' words without knowing their correct meaning. He was in a relationship with a middle-aged woman and, in general, much more experienced than I. He had a wide range of acquaintances and friends, some of whom I did meet in due course. While Wilfried opened many doors for me by meeting people, he had no "spiritual" or mental influence. His misnomers actually caused a certain disrespect. This is why, after a few years, I lost contact with him.

One of his friends was Hannelore Tuberg. My age, she was at the time involved with a 45+ year old American professor and at times traveled with him. She, herself, taught English at a local school. Smart she was, but also promiscuous. She had had a brother by the name of Herbert, who had died of, to me, unknown causes. Since I had a sister by the name of Hannelore, this coincidence was of a minor importance to her. Through her, I became acquainted with Beethoven's music. And not only with him, but American service men, one of whom introduced me to pizza, etc., etc.

She also had a private English student by the name of Friderike Obee, a 24 year old, tall, very attractive, classy female of a

223

more southern appearance. She definitely did not fit my ideal of the northern blonde. In short, she was out of my range. I got to know her by Hannelore asking one day if I could drive her home to Nordenstadt outside Wiesbaden, which the three of us did. Then we had some other outing together, from which I drove Ika, as she was called, home in the evening. Well, the woman just wouldn't get out of my car – actually my father's, I had ready access to. So, in order to be able to get home, I knew I had to kiss her just to get her out of my car. I did. And that was the beginning of my first hot relationship. But "she danced only one summer". I was not in her league. Apparently there were plans for her to marry a Diplomingenieur (Certified Engineer). I may have been a fling before the final commitment. When I learned of the good bye, I was devastated. And I don't think it was easy on her either. Never was I able to look behind the scene of what had been going on. From Hannelore I later learned, that the marriage had quickly dissolved and happening to meet her younger brother at a gas station, I was told that Ika had gone to Lisbon in Portugal. Much, much later did I try to track her down through the Internet, but with women changing last names, it is virtually impossible.

By that time, the late summer of 1957, I had decided to go to engineering school in Bingen, figuring that I could never get anywhere as a draftsman. Thus I left my job at M.A.N. once more. But I was moping and whenever our instructor connected the geometry point o to b, Obee in German, I jerked up. I also established that I surely must have a general deficiency in math skills, a prerequisite for an engineer. After two and one half months exposure at this school, I quit. Devastated again! But an important insight I gained at engineering school, where we had also, I can't really recall, something like religious studies or philosophy. Our instructor told of two philosophical orientations: To be "diesseits" or "jenseits" oriented, to think in terms of "the here and now" or "the beyond". I knew then, that my orientation was in the here and now!

At that time my uncle Fritz arranged to have me tested, for intelligence and aptitude, by a psychologist. I recall that my math IQ was 98, but my spacial perception 146. Quite a range. From below average to genius level. My writing ability tested out second best. The average of the five areas I was tested in gave me a decent 123. Yes, I was able to count at least 1 - 2 - 3!

I continued to get together with my platonic friend, Hannelore. And through her step father I found work at the engineering firm in Wiesbaden where he was employed. A few months into this engagement, I was asked by my superiors whether I would transfer temporarily to their Hamburg office. This I did and got to know a bit of Germany's north. At the hotel I stayed, one of the bar maids took to me and I had my first "you know what". Quickly thereafter I returned to Wiesbaden and within a short time left Dorsch-Gehrmann. I found work at another small Wiesbaden company.

The question was still: How can I advance in life? I decided to try it by improving my language skills and to add French to it. My father was able to secure an offer of work as a designateur, a draftsman, with the French subsidiary, Société des Ponts & Travaux en Fer, of a German company in Paris. This was to be for a six months period. Well, aside from two years Latin, repeated once, I had no knowledge of Romance languages. So I took first one, than another French course at Berlitz. In the first course I began dating a girl by the name of Heidi von Schweitzer. While she was nice, she wasn't really attractive. And once she expressed, that she wanted to have five children, I skipped. One evening, from the follow-up class, I invited another girl for a drink. We may have had two, and in the process of leaving the rather empty bar I learned in a doorway the enormous gyrating flexibility of a female's lower torso. She turned out to be the wildest, most aggressive female I have ever come across. It did not take long to dissolve this relationship, although, in later years, it would have been great fun.

If the reader, by now, has not yet comprehended what was going on, then... Back from North Africa I had exploded outward, trying all kinds of relationships and employment, the latter improving my income. The years between 20 and 24 were, in many ways, my most aggressive ones.

Well, and then my platonic friendship with Hannelore Tuberg changed when, following an abortion, she needed more than a

225

comforting word. Against my better knowledge I let Eros enter. But that fell also into the time of my departure for Paris on December 1, 1958. That, fortunately, put a damper on this relationship. While I traveled a few times back and forth during the 10 months I spent in total in Paris, I also had many visitors, so that I had a regular tour I took these people on. I lived in a hotel on Rue de Navarin, not far from Rue Pigalle, or Pig Alley, as postwar American troops called this street, accommodation paid by my employer.

The company employed about 40 people in various rooms of a city house. It had a small refectory where lunches were catered in every day for those employees wishing to participate. These were three-course meals with vin ordinaire, the latter cut with water in a percentage according to the diner's liking. That's where I also learned for the first time to eat artichokes, was advised by one of my sophisticated colleagues, actually a displaced Pole, to pluck out the inside leaves, the fuzz, then pour oil and vinager plus salt and pepper into the opening and – voila – having a continuous dressing dispensed when eating the leaves from the inside out.

The house employed also a concierge, an Alsacien, who had grown up while the Alsace was part of Germany until the end of WW1. He enjoyed speaking German with me and addressed me with the antiquated form of "Ihr" and "Euch". I almost felt like royalty.

Since I got my main meal at the company, I needed something in the evening. This usually consisted of a small baguette I picked up on the way "home" to the hotel and often some Jambon de Westphalie from a butcher shop, run by a madame who reminded me by her stout built of my mother. When I entered, she always knew what I wanted. And since I had no means of refrigeration at my hotel room, it was bread and ham, no butter. I was paid once a month. So I had to budget. I usually send home to Germany in moneys whatever I figured not to need. This worked most of the time, except when an "emergecy" arose, like my watch conking out. Then there was no Jambon de Westphalie, but La Vache Qui Rit, the Laughing Cow spreading cheese.

I worked in a room with four Frenchmen. There was our boss, who's name I've forgotten. Then there was Louis Lemarié, we called grand père because of his age, able to doze off at times on his four-poster drawing board, Marcel Petuaud and Michel Mauduit, the latter two avowed communists, I very much debated and told: You are not going to win. I was proved right 30 years later!

Grand père and Marcel invited me to their homes for dinner a few times, where I was introduced to the delights of French cooking and spirits. Grand père had two unmarried daughters, older than I, who did the cooking. Following a dinner that had started with an aperitif, then an appetizer with a white wine, a salad, the main course with, maybe, a red wine, followed by a desert, then a digestive, grand père usually suggested to go for a walk in a nearby park. There, he soon desired to rest on a bench, where he fell promptly asleep.

In the spring of 1961 Ute and I spent our "honeymoon" in Paris – my connections were still fresh at the time. The Petuauds invited us for dinner. A couple of years later, when they traveled to Tchechoslovakia – it was still one country then – and under communist rule, they stopped by in our Watzhahn apartment. What to serve them for dinner? We decided on suckling wild pig with various salads, and it turned out a good intro to German cuisine.

My evenings at the Alliance Française, improving my French, resulted in a friendship with a young Swiss fellow, Otto Schupp, and a Singaporean Chinese Tony Soon Ho (Singapore, at this time was still a British Crown Colony). Soon introduced me to Thai / Vietnamese cooking in Paris with a sumptuous whole fish dinner. The three of us frequented various dance halls. Years later, when we lived in Schaumburg, Otto Schupp, on business in Chicago, visited with us twice. He had married and had two sons. I, too, saw him and his family once when I paid our Zürich office a visit. Then, suddenly, out of the clear blue sky – I was maybe in my early forties, I received notice that he had died. Cause to me – unknown. He barely made it to 40!

Soon, once his stay in Paris had come to an end, visited with us in Germany, staying at our house for two or three weeks, during which time he tried to get a permit to study German. He once cooked a Chinese-Indian dinner for our family, at which time it turned out, that he carried a substantial bag of curry with him, courtesy of his mother in Singapore. During the Japanese invasion of Southeast Asia in WW2 they had lived at various places in India. I recall from one of our many discussions, while he lived with us, that I emphasized the importance of

227

Europe having opened up the planet, had made it in some sense one, a feat never accomplished by any previous culture. He emphasized Chinese inventiveness and dominance of culture – which I acknowledged, but with a more regional impact. When he prepared the above mentioned meal, naturally including rice, he told of an old Chinese saying that: "Every grain of rice not eaten, brings one year of bad luck". And while not one in my family was superstitious, we ate every grain of rice – and did so forever afterwards. Even the kids picked up on it.

He also conveyed to us a family story. His sister had gone to London for studies. There, at the university, she fell in love with a Dutchman and wanted to marry him. Her parents were strongly against the relationship, because she was going to marry below her ethnic status, Chinese! She did anyway. Her parents cut her off and for years there was no communication. Then, somehow, they reconnected in Singapore, and her parents were able to accept her Caucasian husband.

A few times I visited with the Klages family in Fontainebleau, south of Paris where, at the time the NATO headquarters were still located. Rolf Klages, the son of Karl Klages, who vacationed with us one year in Bavaria, was delegated there by the German military. With their daughter, Inge, the same age as my sister, and good friends with her, we one day even won a live duck at a village market. This was a family friendship, that covered three generations. And, who knows, at some point more might have transpired. On September 30, 1959 I returned to Wiesbaden.

But briefly back to my last employment at M.A.N. During this stint I had become friends with a two year older engineer, who had been a FDJ (Free Democratic Youth) functionary in East Germany's communist youth movement. He had grown tired of it and had fled to West Germany which, in 1956 was still possible. He became my most important friend and we did many things together, among which was another trip to Sweden in 1958. (In 1957 I traveled with my father on a coastal steamer from Bremen through the Ostseekanal up the Swedish west coast to Oslo and back and experience a storm of magnitude six on the 600 ton ship). Horst Nitschke together with Wilfried Wolf were to be the most influential friends of these years. It is interesting to note here, that I should remember Horst's full name because he was my "Idea supplier", while I can barely recall Wolf's name, who helped me make people connections. Both were a few years older, a trend I had followed already in previous years in the selection of friends, and transmitted plenty of knowledge to me. This, my preference, made me stretch myself, challenged me, and enriched my learning I had missed at school.

Horst, in many ways, had a sharp mind, but was socially a bit inept, particularly with women. That did not prevent him, though, from establishing some liaisons. One, in the winter of 1960, resulted in four of us, he, with his girlfriend, and I with Hannelore Tuberg, to venture for New Year to Paris. We stayed at my "old haunt", Hotel des Navarins et des Angleterres. It was a bit of a screwy trip, affair, relationship, etc. On the way home we stopped by at the Klages family in Fontainebleau for an enjoyable visit. Later that year I tried to travel to Spain with Horst's then ex-girlfriend.

For many years Horst lived in Mainz, renting a small souterrain apartment from his landlady, who also had a young daughter. Together with assorted friends we sometimes spent time at Horst's pad and in the garden of the substantial villa. Once we had a get-together at Wilfried Wolf's abode in Mainz, not too far from Horst's place – Wilfried was married by then. Somehow, fooling around, I had snatched Horst's car key, but he disappeared with his car nevertheless, having a second key taped to the vehicle somewhere. I wasn't yet done with Horst, though. Wilfried and I drove to Horst's place, where we found his car parked outside. Using my towrope and his key, we towed the car about midnight across the Rhine bridge to my place in Biebrich, about 6 km. It must be said here, that Wilfried Wolf, who steered the towed vehicle, had no driver's license! Next day Horst, a silly grin on his face, appeared at our house in Biebrich to fetch his car. Well, at least he got a dinner at our place out of it.

Somewhere in my report I mention, that Horst became employed at the engineering offices of Ehrhardt, my ex-employer. Not long after my departure from there, Mr. Ehrhardt closed his offices and assumed a job with a larger company. Horst was able to secure representation for two of the Ehrhardt suppliers for himself. He was sitting pretty. But then he got his landlady's daughter, by that time not that young any more, pregnant. Marriage was called for – by mother and daughter. And what followed was sad. It appears that the two women really took him to the cleaners. Before that evolved, he had a daughter and, if I'm not mistaken, a son. Horst began to drink! Eventually a divorce happened – all while we were in Canada, between 1964 and 1970. In the early seventies, when we lived in Schaumburg, he used to call us several times a week, frequently intoxicated, to chat about his problems. Then this stopped. It turned out, that his business activities had suffered, and he had lost both representations. He had moved into an apartment in the Rhine-Main area. I had lost some touch with him, although in the first years, before the slide, I paid him a visit here and there, but my sister Hannelore kept kind of track of him. A downhill slide seemed to take place, from what she reported. Eventually, he seemed to have moved again, but the question arose, whether he had committed suicide!

This all bothered me quite a bit, and on a visit to Germany, it must have been in the early eighties, I wanted to track him down. So I drove to Mainz and rang the bell at the door of his former landlady. A girl, maybe in her late teens, answered the door and I introduced myself. Although I had never made her acquaintance, she knew instantly who I was! Upon my explanation that I wanted to find her father, and whether she could tell me his address, she told me, obviously in German: "I have no contact with my Pappi any more!" But she gave me Horst's address in a little town in the Rhine-Main area, across the river.

That same day I drove there, but no one answered my ring. I tried the next day and Horst opened the door. Interestingly, my expressions of concern for him, caused him to be concerned for my concern. But we settled down and were able to converse about his fate. He had been ill, had no job, but looked basically okay, and also stated, that he was doing all right. That was enough for me. I had closure and could let go. It was the last time I saw or heard from him!

230

Another friendship that evolved at my workplace was with an (oriental) Indian, dark as an African, but with somewhat Caucasian features. Although having a diploma in engineering (a master's degree), he was made to work for me, a mere draftsman, when he joined the M.A.N. company. So much for respect and ethnic acceptance in the late 50s in Germany! We became good friends, did many things together, and I learned of a different culture, just as I had from Tony Soon Ho, from Singapore. From both I learned, that ethnic intolerance and prejudice cuts across all races, not by them personally, but their families at home.

Milton Guha, aka Surajit Kumar Guha Thakurta, from Calcutta, my Indian friend, had left India for studies in England. He had worked for a British company, thereafter moved to Germany and worked for a small pump company. After that he had arrived at M.A.N., where I met him. While, at the beginning, see above, he was discriminated against, he later worked his way up, becoming the M.A.N.s pump department outside representative. This happened after I had left the country. Whenever I returned for visits, I visited with him and his wife, a German. Eventually they had a daughter. He built a house near Mainz and acquired German citizenship! They used to spend their vacations in the east of Europe, Romania, the Black Sea coast, and Turkey. Asked for their reason, they said, that they did not encounter racial prejudice there. Because of their mixed-race marriage they also stated, that they would never visit the United States they considered racist – in the early 80s. At the time I tried to convince them, that this was more true in certain areas then others, but to no avail. While I could understand their concern to some extent it, nevertheless, put a crimp in our relationship, for then I would always be the one visiting them, but they never me / us. Then M.A.N. closed its pump department and, as I learned later, Milton joined another pump manufacturer, Halberg Machinenbau GmbH, in Ludwigshafen, Germany. I made one futile attempt to track them down. Alas...

At times I also invited sales trainees from other countries to my parent's home. These men spent a few days or weeks at the M.A.N. department where I worked. I first asked my parents if that was okay, then the guys what food restrictions they might have. Then my mother would cook a meal according to that.

We had an open house! My parents put no restrictions on me, maybe they sometimes wondered about the kinds of people I "dragged" in. But having the grocery store, many skippers traveling the Rhine, used to stop overnight at Biebrich, just off the store, to purchase their supplies there. Some became friends and stopped for more than groceries.

One of those skippers, his last name was Vohwinkel, was an almost regular guest. One evening, supper finished, my parents kept chatting with him into the night. I was drifting in and out of the room. I had my own. "Chewing the fat" over some Rhine wine, Vohwinkel, at some point had to visit the loo. Quickly my mother took his glasses and smeared them with a thin film of butter from the butter dish still standing on the table. The skipper came back, put on his glasses again, and never said a word. Now you see what too much Rhine wine can do.

That's how we also acquired coal in the dark of the night in the immediate postwar years when everything was scarce. I recall shoveling coal into sacks in a tug's hold, then loading it with my father on a four-wheel cart and rushing up the street to cover up our illegal venture. That's another feature of my family, though. Even in the worst of times – but we were also lucky during and after the war – we had a knack to supply ourselves with necessities. I have always recalled my mother's admonition, moving her left index finger first along the length of her right one, saying: That much selling is better – at that time she moved her left index finger from the tip of the right one to the crook of the elbow – than that much working. I've always taken that to heart!

One other important thing! Although my father had been a minor member of the NAZI party, and mom's mother supposedly lost a house through a Jewish money lender, they never foisted any prejudices on me. I was free to grow up as I choose! I am forever grateful to them, for this enabled me later to pass on that same lack of ethnic prejudice to my children. I think.

A reflection: Am I talking too much? Am I too frank at times? Do I miss issues? But I think it lies in these details of life, that I came to be who I am. And there's lots more I'd rather not enter into.

8. Trouble ahead

Then, in the spring of 1960 my friend Horst had dissolved a relationship. I knew his girlfriend. And I had plans for next year to do a trip with my car to Spain. By that time I had bought my father's Beetle. I was looking for companionship and expense sharing. So, I approached her. First she wanted, but when I tested what the relationship could be like, she didn't want to go to Spain. Now I needed to find other companions and spread the word accordingly.

By that time my cousin Fritz and Ute had married, much to my regret. I still recall my sorrow, when I bid them good bye in the hallway of his father's residence, thinking: Here goes a good party – thinking only of Ute. But I figured it was a done deal. The two moved into a small souterrain apartment in the north of Biebrich. I, being into all and everything at the time, thought to bring some life into their, what I perceived rather "drab" existence. So, together with my Indian friend Milton I, at times, showed up at weekends to do things together. I soon gained a vague sense that not all was well in this young marriage. And I still liked Ute very much.

Well, in this context I mentioned also my desire to travel to Spain and that I was looking for companions. And so it happened that Fritz and Ute, but also Ute's cousin, Renate, agreed to come along. And off we went in late summer of 1960, traveling through southern France to Biarritz, in the Bay of Biscaine, visiting the Caves of Altamira, to get into Madrid. Next day, at the Prado, I stood in front of Francisco Goya's haunting painting "The Third of May, 1808", the execution of Spanish resistance fighters by Napoleonic troops. It left an indelible impression on me. Entering Madrid, a dragger guided us to the hotel he was working for, and we got the newlywed suite. Who knows – had Renate there been agreeable – who knows how life would have turned out and troubles have been avoided. Down to Malaga we drove and up the coast to Barcelona. Just north of it we found nice accommodation in a little seaside place, a small cove, called Tamariu. We enjoyed good food, good and cheap spirits, and one night I got carried away and bit, yes bit, the two women on various appendages and otherwise. Fritz did not like this at all, particularly not on his wife. Then he fell ill from a

233

stomach disorder and was room-bound. I do recall sitting on the cove's rocks, having the heads of the two women resting in my lap, the surf hitting just below, I humming jazz rhythms. When Fritz had recovered, things between him and Ute stood not at their best. I recall them standing high on the cliff above us, Renate and I (head on lap) on the beach, and being obviously in disagreement.

And then and there I made the audacious prediction to Renate: "Within a year Ute and I will be married!" Well, if a few family members would hear this, most of them are gone by now, I would be "guilty as charged"! And, maybe, I am. In later years I have sometimes wondered whether I am a truly immoral s.o.b. But I wouldn't want to insult my mother! Maybe I have been that at times. But if I learned something from my early fantasy years and their disastrous ending, it was: If you want something, you gotta go for it! You also have to work for it, hard (or subtly). If anything shaped me, it is this insight, and it stood me well through the years into the present. Yet, this hard-won approach also had its cost! Maybe I was impatient before in my early years, but I cannot recall this. To get where I needed to go, to get what I wanted, I had become impatient with myself and, regretfully, with others. To succeed, I had to go for things. More about that later.

9. Into the Maelstrom

We returned from Spain, each to his or her own devices. I kept working at M.A.N.'s pump engineering department, well aware that I would be unable to properly support a hypothetical family on the salary achievable in this kind of work. I entertained thoughts that I would eventually inherit some wealth from my parents, but found these thoughts reprehensible, too far in the future, and not relying on the self. So I searched newspaper ads looking for evening work in my field of drafting expertise. Anything, anything to make a buck, actually a deutschmark, to at least supplement my income. And I did find such work – and very well paid.

Soon, the owner, Mr. Ehrhardt, offered me full-time employment in his engineering office with twice the salary I made at M.A.N. Unnecessary to say: I jumped for it. I was his first full-time employee. He represented several companies in the southern part of the state of Hesse. At first I produced drawings for industrial projects. Then, it so happened, that one of the companies he represented had an industrial and an agricultural section. At the time the German federal government was pumping money into agriculture to make farms operate more effectively. That often meant for a farmer to relocate from the confines of the village he lived in out into the midst of his acreage. In any case, farmers upgraded their milk cow stalls with new neck restraints and manure conveyors, silage silos, etc. And very quickly I slipped into such sales.

All the while things between Ute and Fritz deteriorated – even without my interference. However, I must have also helped it along by showing up at their place. Then they split. Ute and I read stories to each other. I recall some were from John Steinbeck's 'Red Pony'. We hung out together surreptitiously or not so surreptitiously. I also began writing little poems for Ute:

Love

When shall it be	Quand sera-t-il
the cry of gulls	le cri des mouettes
the play of wind	das Spiel des Windes
like fingers in your hair	wie Finger in deinem Haar
a whispering of trees	a whispering of trees
I love you	je t'aime
the knowledge of grapes	ein Wissen der Trauben
I drink you	je te bois
arms golden in sunlight	Arme golden I'm Sonnenlicht
stars	Sterne
you and me	toi et moi
here or anywhere	here or anywhere
never - once - or forever	jamais - une foi - ou toujours

Hope / Hoffen

Terribly wonderful the days	Schrecklich schön die Tage
when one knows	da man weiß
knowing in the i=unknown	wissend I'm Ungewissen
waiting for tomorrow	warned auf morgen
fearing what barely won	fürchtend kaum Erworbene
to lose	zu verlieren
and hoping, hoping, and	und hoffen, hoffen, und
dreaming	träumen
damned impatience	verdammte Ungeduld
damned dreaming	verdammtes Träumen
think of now	denk an jetzt
and trust in tomorrow	und vertrau auf morgen

At one time I was asked by Fritz to stay away, but refused. That didn't help. Then, one evening, walking up there, I made, or had made my decision. This is it. I want to "have" Ute. And that was it! Not long thereafter Ute filed for divorce. She was actually somewhat uneasy with me. From the "living corpse" I seemed to have become a little too much. Anyway, she was in agreement. And when the divorce had gone through, I asked her to legally change back to her maiden name, Rutkowsky. I didn't want to marry her with my mother's family name, Michels. This happened on the 8th of July 1961.

Lo and behold, I had acquired a well-paying job right when I needed it. While Ute still lived in an apartment in Wiesbaden, I asked her one evening: Can I buy a new car? Her response: It looks like it. So I purchased a new VW beetle. Two weeks later she found she was pregnant. And then our son, Dirk Uwe, was born two weeks prematurely on December 25, 1961.

Obviously, by that time family relation had gone from bad to worse. Fritz's family cut off contact with my parents, a state that was maintained for years to come. My mother was the one to suffer most from this. But when I had told them of the pregnancy and that we were going to marry, I / WE HAD THEIR SUPPORT!

We found a neat apartment in a 200 soul community, Watzhahn, just beyond the Taunus mountains, about 26 km from Wiesbaden, overlooking the Taunus range from the back. Somewhat similar to how we nowadays overlook the Bradshaw mountains 10,000 km farther west.

Shortly after we were married, I had this premonition, that something was going to happen to me. And it did. On one of my sales trips, approaching a farming village after a slight drizzle with roads being slick, particularly were farmers had entered the roadway with their tractors coming from the muddy fields, I suddenly saw a small car ahead of me. He was practically in the middle of the road backing up for whatever reason. It was, what was then called a Leucoplast Bomber, a Band-Aid bomber, the body a plastic material, everything lightweight. I hit the brakes, my head on the windshield, and the rear of the other vehicle. My beetle was slightly flattened up front. The other vehicle didn't look so good. We were both getting out and then the police came. It turned out that a bolt holding the spare tire inside the rammed car had come loose and had hit the back of the other driver's head. He was bleeding slightly. I got a citation, was convicted, of bodily injury, and had to pay a fine of DM70, maybe $20 at the time. I pulled out the right front fender of my VW and was able to drive home. This has been my only "serious" accident in my entire driver's life. But I now had "a record", as minor as it was, for 10 years in the German traffic annals in Flensburg.

Five years later, when we applied for immigration to the US, I had checked off "no previous convictions" in the questionnaire, since my records from Germany did not list the above event. Well, when I was called for a final review by the US immigration officer in Toronto, he went down the list and when he arrived at "previous convictions" asked me: "Would you like to reconsider your response here?" And that was it. I entered the United States with a conviction for bodily injury. The FBI must have known, however, how minimal it was, that Immigration let me pass.

Sometimes, Ute and Dirk came along on one of my sales excursions in Hesse. Ahead of a village, I dropped them off and Ute went into the woods collecting mushrooms, which we then consumed in the evening. And she endeared herself to me, among other things, by putting together little moss plates, collections from the woods surrounding us. Walking across the fields and meadows, I could ask her to find a four-leafed clover – and unfailingly she would.

Yet, what seemed to be with every cough of mine, she got pregnant. But before the next child was due, but Ute being pregnant again – she practically always was then – her parents came visiting from Indonesia to inspect that come-along son-in-law, but also to baby-sit Dirk, so that Ute and I could vacation in Sweden and Norway, I had fallen in love with. I showed Ute some of my old haunts in Sweden, but we also traveled to some new country north of Oslo and stayed in a cabin, part of a vacation lodge in a national park. It was midsummer, and we left one evening to hike up onto a nearby mountain. Once past the tree line we were in tundra-like open country all the way to the

238

peak, and all with plenty of light still. Our trail-less descent brought us to the tree line again, where I expected to pick up the trail back down to the lodge. We walked first one direction along the forest's edge, then the other. No trail! How could it have disappeared? Well, we just didn't walk far enough along the forest's edge!

Then, with a five months pregnant wife, I descended through the forest – and a very boggy forest it was – always following the sound of the river below us. It must have been 2:00 o'clock in the morning we arrived at our cabin. But we also had the most delicious, freshly caught salmon at the lodge, so good, that I asked them for another like meal.

And soon Kirsten came along, she even being a premie six weeks early, on November 12, 1962, two days after Ute's 26th birthday, the 10th of November. By hat time I had purchased another, bigger car, and shortly thereafter another bigger one yet. We had it good – but I got itchy – again. It was fine to have it good, but I had traveled and missed new sights. Before all these pregnancies, we had thought of taking a bus which, at that time, traveled from London to Calcutta. Alas... One evening, walking across the fields – we had an elderly couple as occasional baby-sitters, living above us, I asked her: "Would you go to some other country with me?" And without hesitation my intrepid wife said: Yes!

10. Adventure calling

Thus, I began inquiring for jobs overseas. One, in sales, would have taken us to Lagos, Nigeria, God forbid. Another, as a draftsman, to Euratom at the Swiss-Italian border. Neither materialized. Then my father pointed out an ad in an engineering magazine in which a technician's position was offered to set up service facilities at the Canadian sister company for Canada and the USA. I knew the German parent company, Kuhlmann. I had worked on their drafting equipment for years. I wanted that job! Gosh, Canada and the US, what a way to go! I applied, was invited for an interview to Wilhelmshaven, returned home and immediately wrote a follow-up letter, expressing my strong desire and qualification for the job. I had experience in sales, ha, to farmers mostly, I had technical experience, and I spoke English and French. What more could Kuhlmann want! I was asked once more to come up to meet my visiting future boss – and was hired. And then I had to convey - carefully - that Ute was pregnant with a third child, Karen, who saw the light on the 17th day of November 1963. And since this multiplication could not go on forever, Ute was exhausted, her tubes were tied. Having missed a period, she may have already been pregnant again. The routine scraping of the uterus prior to the tubeligation may have saved her / us from another pregnancy which, according to her gynecologist's advice, would have been detrimental to Ute's exhausted health and the forthcoming emigration.

I had left Ingenieurbüro Ehrhardt, but only months after I had brought in my friend Horst Nitschke as a second full-time employee, and we gave up our apartment in Watzhahn, with the family temporarily moving in with my parents.

To further improve my English I wanted to take private lessons, and with Ute's agreement I contacted Hannelore Tuberg, introduced the two, and took my lessons - English only. Once in Wilhelmshaven, I took further lessons from an Englishman.

My superiors-to-be accepted the third child in good humor?, and on January 2, 1964 I shipped up to Wilhelmshaven, in between also to their secondary plant in Bad Lauterberg, in the Harz Mountains, for four months of training and introduction to their equipment. I had taken the train to get to Kuhlmann/Wilhelmshaven. My father had bought my Opel Rekord car. In Wilhelmshaven I had to walk a lot; it is a sprawling city, originally created from three different communities. Within a few weeks I developed a terrible pain inside the front of my right foot, causing me to limp along. Then I had to go to Bad Lauterberg for two weeks of training on their machine tools. It still hurt! Ute was to come up for a brief visit – Lauterberg isn't that far from Wiesbaden, three hours by car. It had snowed that night and was bitter cold. Her arrival by train was about 3:00 in the morning. I missed my alarm call by a few minutes, dressed hurriedly and took a shortcut through some alleys to the train station. The train had just pulled out! I hurried back – the official way – and found Ute in tears in front of the door no one had opened in the bitter cold. Ah, what contrition!

Then, the beginning of May we flew out to Canada after I convinced the company that it was "cheaper" than getting us over by boat. And, would you believe it: A Lufthansa ground hostess at Montreal airport, it turned out, had been a girlfriend of my boss-to-be. Small world again.

We arrived in a new world, The New World, and were put up for a couple of weeks in a cottage motel with all the conveniences. Out on the lawn bopped the Robins. The German-born service manager, Helmut Dietrich, helped us to get settled. After two weeks we moved into a townhouse on Barsuda Drive in Clarkson, a township later incorporated into the larger city of Mississauga.

In a small container some of our furniture had come with us from Germany. But it was by far not enough for a complete and comfortable home. I made bookshelves and beds for the children from discarded Kuhlmann crates. Well, it turned out, we had stepped down far below the income and conveniences we had had in Germany! I would say, it took us about ten years to get back to a similar living standard. Sure, two years later we owned our own house, and six years down the road we had a big company car, but that was yet to come. In the meantime, what one could call, the daily conveniences, going out for a dinner, being able to buy this and that, etc. were much reduced.

It turned out, that our sales manager, Dave Wishart, lived in the same complex. And quickly we became friends with an American couple of the same age in the adjacent unit, Paul and Carolyn Harrington. Ute and Carolyn became fast friends and Paul worked hard to make an American out of me by introducing me to football, baseball, basketball, and golf – without success. He had been transferred by his US-parent company for a two-year stint in Canada. This friendship was utterly important for Ute, who had lost her support system, meager even in Germany – her parents were still in Indonesia. The Dietrichs helped here and there.

On all future annual trips, mostly for business, I arranged to fly out of Toronto, or later Chicago, on a Thursday arriving in Frankfurt on Friday morning. From there it was just a short hop to Wiesbaden, where I stayed with my parents and sister. Then, on Sunday afternoon I took off for either Bad Lauterberg or Wilhelmshaven. If it was to be Wilhelmshaven, I used to stop over, staying over night with Ute's parents in Helmenzen, in the Westerwald. In the first years of my employment with Kuhlmann Impex, as it was originally called, I had to take the trains to visit Kuhlmann when my dad was still working and needed his car. Once he had retired, which happened in 1971, he lent me his car to get around in Germany. Before this, my parents often used to drive up to Bad Lauterberg, while I spent time there, and we toured the Harz Mountains and looked at the fortified border fence separating East from West Germany at the time.

On my first return trip to Germany in 1965 I learned that Hannelore Tuberg had married and was practically living next door in the town of Schierstein. I called, to say hello, and was invited to stop by. She was happily pregnant. Her rather boyish-looking husband stayed mostly in the background during my visit.

The Harringtons also introduced us to Sandy Lake, a small lake north of Peterborough. Together, we rented two cottages and spent a week there. Ute had saved some money from the household funds to make it possible. That reminds me of something connected. My income was poor. Household money was dear. Carolyn advised Ute to put $20 into four envelopes – and those $20 dollars had to last for a week each.

From household money savings she was also able to divert $5 a month to pay off a black and white TV, in the process establishing Credit. The Harringtons had a big color TV and there we were introduced to some of the TV fare from across the border, the USA. Paul was a Budweiser quaffer. From time to time he got up to relieve himself and continue. Never did he appear drunk. He only fell asleep later in the evening, particularly when his wife had temporarily gone back to Ohio to give birth to additional children to the two they already had. Then we would tiptoe back out to our pad next door. On a hot summer's day – we had no air conditioning – both Paul and Dave Wishart, had been temporarily forsaken by their wives. We invited them for dinner and had really hot stuffed banana peppers on rice. For years our talks came back at times to this tasty, but rather sweaty experience.

I frequently had to leave for business trips, sometimes for 4-5 weeks at a time, making the circuit of the USA, getting into Mexico City and Canada. Ute had to fend for herself. We had bought an old Peugeot and eventually she got her drivers license. Before joining Kuhlmann I had once been on a short flight in a Piper aircraft over Stuttgart and had enjoyed it very much. But now, that I had to fly in big, commercial airplanes I was very much afraid. In these "tubes", delivered to an unknown pilot, I felt to have lost all control over my existence. Through my mother I obtained some Valium and took it whenever I flew. Never did I hide this, at times mentioning it to fellow-travelers, and through this openness learned of how very much others were affected. Once, a man told he, that he had five drinks at the airport to enable him to fly.

Then, on one of my returns from Los Angeles to Toronto, I missed my connecting flight from Chicago to Toronto due to overbooking. Air Canada brought in an additional plane to accommodate the large number of people that had gathered that evening. Then we took off in a full Vickers Viscount four-engine turboprop. On my flights I had always chosen one of the window-exit seats. Upon our landing approach to Toronto I heard the repeated bumps of the wing landing gear on my side attempting to come out. Being a technician I knew what that meant and that we were in trouble. Well, we circled for a couple of hours to use up excess fuel while the airport authorities foamed the runway. Then we came in, straight as an arrow, on the nose gear and the right wing wheels. It was interesting to see the props bending backwards and the sparks flying. Coming to a stop, I opened the window exit and was the first one out of the damned plane. Ute was waiting with the children in the lobby to take me home. Never were they told what had been going on in the sky and on the tarmac. Following this experience, I decided I had to be able to fly without Valium, and I have done so ever since. And I've crossed the Atlantic more than 70 times, the Pacific a dozen times, not counting the many other flights across the US and those in Africa.

On one of my first business trips to Houston in 1965, where our US head office was located at the time, I met Willy Liesner, regional sales manager, and a couple of years older than I. He had, among other things, worked as an electrician in the nickel mines in Sudbury, Ontario, before joining Kuhlmann-Impex in his current position in Houston. On a night-drive from Dallas to Houston, after a day of sales calls – my function on these trips was technical support of sales people – he told me that he wanted to become a millionaire. I gasped. Having just come from Germany, thoughts of this nature were rather uncommon at the time, particularly with my now meager salary of CAN$ 550.00. Until these days we have kept in touch, having become friends. He wanted to hire me twice as manager of small companies he acquired in the course of his advance, and both times I declined. Once, when we met in Houston he introduced me to his partner: "This is Herb Windolf. He's a son of a bitch, but he's a good man." As good as he was, Willy that is, I felt some distance was better – for me. In the early 1970s we even considered buying Kuhlmann America Inc. together, as it was then called, but the new managing director at Kuhlmann in Germany, Heinz Lossie, didn't want to part with the profitable dependency. More about that later.

Willy went his way to become a multimillionaire. When, later, during one of our chance meetings – he had left Kuhlmann, of course – no way to get rich at Kuhlmann (yet, maybe after all!), he egged me on by saying: "Do you want to live off Social Security when you're old?" Eventually, Willy moved back to Europe, representing a company almost worldwide, then settled in Munich. But he had acquired a chunk of property to become a nursery in Houston as well as a townhouse, and shuttled back and forth between the two domiciles. Then, in 2000, he wanted to celebrate his 66th birthday. For this event he entertained about 125 people for three days, a hundred of which had flown in from Germany, the rest from the US and Canada. I flew in too. For the occasion I tried to honor him with a poem I wrote for him, and him alone: Paean to a Friend

I'll have to hop back and forth from now on, for life became "denser". While we lived in Canada, my title had been Head, Technical Operations. My boss and I, another German, didn't quite see eye to eye. Once a year I had to travel to our two plants in Germany for additional training or consultations. After two years renting the townhouse we thought it time to buy a house. We found a four bedroom newly built place for CAN$19,900 and purchased it with $100 in cash, all we had, and a $2,000 loan from my company, practically a second mortgage. My sister had always lived with my parents, and I wanted her to become more independent, to get "out of the house". Thus, we had invited her to live with us for a time. And for about a year she did, working at a couple of jobs. This enabled Ute to work also at times. At first picking apples and other produce for a nearby farm market, later moving into more responsible tasks at this place. Time permitting, I joined her in apple picking and asparagus cutting – for $1.00/hour, all to supplement our income and to faster pay off the company loan. From our home at 501 Forestwood Drive in Burlington, we became friends with three families across the street, the women all being nurses.

We really latched on to one particular family, Warner and Audrey Clark. We all liked each other. They had two boys, the age of our kids. But something was wrong there already. After we got to know each other better Audrey mentioned: "When the boys are grown, we will get a divorce." That was a few years down the road. Eventually, they did and, while a few visits took place, eventually we lost contact with them.

In 1969 Kuhlmann was to open another office in Chicago, intending to move the somewhat outlying Houston office closer to the center of commercial activity. I was offered the position of sales manager at the new Chicago facility. It meant a higher salary and a big

245

company car. I sure jumped on it. Thus we applied for immigration to the United States which, at the time, was still easier than it became in subsequent years. When, in the course of our application, we were all checked out by a doctor in Toronto, he pointed out an irregularity in Karen's heartbeat and suggested to have it checked in Chicago. Then, first I went to the Windy City (so named for its past windy politics, not for the winds) for business purposes and to look for houses, then Ute flew in one time to make sure I found the right one. And we bought a place on 1708 Cambourne Lane in Schaumburg, Illinois, a town of about 25,000 in early 1970, about 30 miles northwest of the City. In the four years living in our house on Forestwood, our house there had appreciated enough to purchase the Cambourne place through the equity we had acquired. It was priced somewhere around $37,000. And we settled in there for the next 22 years!

Right after we arrived Karen was checked out for her heart condition, and it was found that she had a quarter-size hole between her heart chambers. In an open-heart surgery this defect was closed with a Dacron patch and from thenon she acquired more stamina.

In the summer of 1971 we drove up to Canada in our company-leased Caprice Classic wagon to join the Clarks in visiting Canada's east, Nova Scotia and the Cabot Trail. There we had our first lobster feast, the women having bought nine lobsters, of which the five kids only ate one. So us poor adults had to consume the remaining eight together with a couple of bottles of white. All that on a camping place with ordinary pliers and utensils. The right place to eat lobster. One day I had caught about five flounders and Warner offered to clean them for our evening dinner, which I happily accepted. A couple of days later we went cod-fishing on a small boat, where most of us intrepid seafarers got seasick, or at least queasy. Ute kept pulling in one cod after another together with some mackerel. Now it was my turn for cleaning, I just couldn't get away from it. And there were lots of fish. Oh, and on one of the solo Windolf excursions up a rotten mountain path, where we had to pad the path with rocks to get over a depression, we ended up with the reverse gear no longer functioning. We made it all the way back to Chicago for the repair.

In 1972 Ute and I drove up to Toronto once more to vacation with Audrey and Warner in Trinidad and Tobago where Audrey charmed a visiting captain of a tugboat to take us on a cruise off the island. On board he supplied us with a fresh-caught fish dinner and miscellaneous coral souvenirs.

11. Falling up the Ladder.

The Kuhlmann management – the company, at the time, had dependencies in Sweden, Austria, Canada, the USA, and Switzerland, with Switzerland being the holding company – had decided in the fall of 1969 to expand and establish an office in Chicago, in addition to the one in Houston. In Canada and the United States ten people each were employed. Kuhlmann's sales program consisted of drafting equipment made in Wilhelmshaven and the engraving machines made in Bad Lauterberg. About 80% of sales were in drafting equipment, the rest in machine tools. A drafting unit, at the time, was priced at about $1,200, a manual engraver at about $3,000, the former needing to be installed, the latter usually being shipped to the customer without further ado.

In Chicago, I now had my beloved boss, Werner Fritsch, breathing down my neck. In my new position as sales manager I had to deal with salesmen who were all older than I. And I had no experience in dealing with people. It wasn't that I couldn't sell, e.g. 100 drawing tables to Newport News Shipyard, or earlier, a big 3D Engraver, new, never sold in Canada, from only our catalog, I being 'just' tech support. It had made our Montreal manager so happy, that he treated me that evening to a sumptuous meal, during which I consumed 5 martinis, 1 beer, and 1 Drambui. The street curb then served me as the guide to walk back to my hotel.

Anyway, back to the US of A. Martinis were popular at the time. Not that I liked them. Too strong. But when I look back at these times, taking customers for lunch, we sometimes had three martinis! Then back to the office, either for more sales talk and demonstration of equipment, or for regular office work. I don't know how I did it. Through the seventies and eighties it was interesting to observe how alcohol consumption changed from hard drinks to wine to soft drinks or Perrier water.

At a high-powered meeting of management, including a couple from the parent and holding company, plus our sales reps, a newly devised company slogan was to be mouthed. I refused! That didn't go down well, particularly since I did it in the presence of my subordinates. By the middle of 1971 – I was now 34 years old – I was

248

in deep doo-doo and floundering in my position, as I found out only later.

However, already in the final quarter of 1969 the economy too was floundering. The good 60s came to an end, and by the latter part of 1971 Kuhlmann/Germany decided that the losses, particularly at the US sister, one month with $6,000 sales and 10 salaries to pay, had been enough, and decided to close the US-operation and severely curtail the Canadian one. My boss bossed both companies.

Did I ever get jittery! Still new in the country, having yet few contacts, what was I to do? I gathered material and proposed to Kuhlmann/Germany how to rescue Kuhlmann America Inc. It was to entail switching sales from the labor-intensive drafting sector to the easier-marketed machine tools. Fortunately, Kuhlmann accepted my proposal. I had always had a good relationship with their managing director, Werner Schacher. They may also have felt a certain responsibility for me and my family, having shipped us out to Canada, then the US, with the condition, that we would have to pay back 1/3 of the transfer cost per year for three years. But I was now actually employed already for seven years. In the US all employees were discharged including my boss, Werner Fritsch. In Canada staff was halved.

I established an office in our family room in Schaumburg, rented some warehouse space at a larger company in Elk Grove Village, and tried to turn things around. K.A.I. was deep in debt for two million Deutschmark owed the parent company, if I recall correctly. At the time, the exchange rate was about 3 to 1, amounting to about $660,000. Except for two write-offs of about $50,000 each, I slowly but surely reduced this indebtedness to zero. Overhead had plummeted with the staff discharge and profits had gone up. Sales now consisted of 80% machine tools and 20% drafting equipment, the opposite of what it had been before. In the heydays Kuhlmann in Wilhelmshaven had employed about 800 people, Bad Lauterberg about 160.

When I started up on my own, that is, I was the only employee left in the US, I had to pick up business mail from the company post office box in Roselle. In 1972 communications was much less evolved as it is nowadays. I established a wire address for Kuhlmann America Inc., in short K.A.I, and arrived in naming it Kairos, the contraction of KAI and Roselle. But its actual meaning, the double entendre was, that Kairos was the ancient Greek god of the fortuitous moment. I needed all the help I could get!

And when I said above "on my own", then that was as it largely was. My next superior was in Germany at the parent company, Mr. Werner Schacher, and I had his trust. Not that I could do as I pleased. I had to supply monthly profit & loss statements, as well as annual ones. But the day to day running of the company was my task. It was almost as if it had been my own company.

Back to the Roselle post office. Schaumburg did not have its own post office yet, so private mail for a number of years was delivered by a carrier. One day, Halloween, getting ready for a costume party, I as an African medicine man, there was a knock at the door. Ute was in the midst of whatever, that prevented her from getting the door. That was my task – being partially painted brown with curlers in my hair to get it to be curly like that of an African. I opened the door, and there stood our young female letter carrier, cracking up hilariously seeing my apparition. And she told the gang at the Roselle post office, thus it took a couple of years for the jokes to subside whenever I had to come to the counter to pick up business mail.

Then came the CNC Engravers, computer-controlled machines. Kuhlmann, at first gave representation to another small US corporation with a line of small CNC engravers. When not much was sold, I was able to pull that in too. I hired a part time electronics man, went to shows and, by that time had moved the K.A.I. warehouse, 2,500 sq.ft with an office, to Schaumburg, about three miles down the road from our house. At first I kept the office at home for convenience. I had also started to do a little bit of buying and reselling used equipment on the side. This enabled us to install air conditioning for our house. At one time I picked up a manual engraver in Kansas City and sold it in Schaumburg. At another time I drove down to Dallas with a manual engraver. In Dallas I picked up some Coors beer to take home which, at the time, was not yet available east of the Mississippi. I always remembered my mother's admonition pointing from finger to elbow!

But I also recall my parents first visit in Schaumburg in the summer of 1972. They had once before visited us in Canada. Fully involved in trying to get K.A.I. on its feet again, I recall coming home from errands and shipments (I had to wait at the Elk Grove warehouse for truckers to pick up my shipments), but still had to do office work. I often waved hello, dashing past them to my office. In this context: I have never believed in working continuously overtime, not for myself, nor for my employees later. At times it may be necessary, but only for a while. One should be able to organize one's work well enough that overtime is rarely required!

In the late seventies my sales rep in southern California, Bob Vlasek, had had a very good year in sales. I arranged for him to get an all-expense-paid trip to Germany with me coming along. We got Werner Schacher's company SL280 Mercedes and traveled through parts of Germany. In Garmisch-Partenkirchen in Bavaria we took lodging in a fancy hotel with a swimming pool and a sauna on the upper floor. When we entered, bare naked, of course, as is customary in liberal Europe, we found a bunch of young fellows, also two women in there. It was a big sauna. Some were from France, some from Scandinavia, and two from Bavaria. Unknowing what was going on we took the topmost tier of benches. The Bavarians introduced us to the interesting custom of pouring Obstler, that's a dry fruit schnapps, over the hot rocks from time to time. It vaporized well, causing Bob and me to quickly descend to a lower-tiered bench. Inhaling vaporized alcohol enters one's system verrry quickly! Then another young couple came in, both in swimsuits – and stayed that way. They turned out to be American.

That evening we went to a small Bavarian restaurant with a huge Kachelofen (tiled oven) in its center. I introduced Bob to some Bavarian specialties for dinner, also some drinks. An accordion player went through all the German sing-along songs and when he finally ran out that evening, came up with a few foreign ones. When he played 'The Yellow Rose of Texas', Bob being from that state, friend Bob was in heaven. And later in the evening, the accordion player still going strong, three quarters of the patrons, including the two of us, were snake-dancing over some chairs and tables through the establishment.

I went to machine tool shows in Chicago and Los Angeles. Usually a service tech from the home company came over to assist me in that demanding process. It was Hans Möhlmann, I subsequently became good friends with. When, in 1974, Kuhlmann asked me to assist their Venezuelan representatives in Caracas with a show, I certainly wanted to do this. Alas, contemporaneous with the Caracas show was my Westec show in Los Angeles. I've always looked for "solutions", always! Solutions are what makes the world go round! Thus, Hans did the L.A. Show, and I flew to Caracas.

These were also the years of the Cold War. Hanging always over our heads was the possibility of a nuclear exchange. What if I was in Germany, when war broke out? How could I get back to my family, provided there was anything worthwhile getting back to? I contemplated ways to get from Germany to Spain and, maybe, northeast Africa to find a way across the Atlantic to the Caribbean, and from there up through, what would be left of the United States. Ah, well, it was a fantasy, and would likely never have been possible. Luckily this threat diminished greatly with the collapse of the Soviet Union in 1989 and German unification.

12. Side Trips.

Karen had by then recovered well from her surgery and we resolved to give her a treat. She was to come along and after Caracas we were to vacation for a few days on Trinidad and mostly Tobago, islands just off the Venezuelan coast. But – in Caracas I had to go to the show! We stayed at the Tamanaco Hotel, the finest in town with a huge garden and pool. The 11 year old kid got the room key, some instructions on what to do and what not, and I went to work. And she made friends at the pool. Some "friends" on her behind, though, were not so kosher. Spending almost all day in her swimsuit by the pool, she developed pimple by pimple on her buttocks. Eventually, I started counting them to check if they kept increasing, or whether the number had stabilized. They were more a nuisance than a pain, and there was little we could do in Caracas. Evenings we had dinner at the hotel, once with a fellow who had just come from prospecting in the jungle, another time with tomato farmers from California, contacts Karen had established.

During our one day stay on Trinidad, we also saw a doctor re the unwelcome pimples. We were asked to enter the MDs office which, very dark, almost hid the dark features of the ethnic Indian MD. He listened extensively to my explanations and I kept wondering: Is he ever going to have a look at this young, white girl's derriere? Finally he did, then said: I'm afraid, I don't know what it is caused by, but gave us the address of a dermatologist-colleague on Tobago. When I asked for his charge he responded: "There's no charge. I couldn't help you!" — Think about that one for a while!

On Tobago we went fishing and I caught a big Barracuda. Pictures were taken. It was funny when we saw them later. When I held the fish, it was relatively small. When Karen held it, it became huge. It was prepared in the hotel's kitchen and served as a fish course for 10 people. I had seen prepared shark jaws and thought: Maybe my Barracuda would make a somewhat smaller, but still nice jaw display. So I asked the cook to save it for me. That afternoon, with a knock at our door, there stood the cook with a big grin and a newspaper-wrapped parcel. "Barracuda jaw, sir." I fished for a tip, but the smallest I could find was five US-dollars. He disappeared immensely happy. When we unwrapped the parcel – there was the multi-hinged jaw with still all the flesh on, which I had expected to be cooked off. Now we had to find a place to dispose of the smelly souvenir. Next day, same time, the room phone rang: "Sir, you want more Barracuda jaw?"

And have you ever cracked a coconut on a beach without any tools, just on and with the rocks available? It's a tough job, but I wanted to show Karen what a coconut is like.

When Dirk had graduated from Junior High, his reward was to be a canoe trip in the Boundary Waters in northern Minnesota, a venture I had never done before. We rented our equipment in Ely, MN, from an outfitter and took off. Fishing was not good. One day, we became stranded for 9 hours on the eastern shore of a lake due to strong incoming winds and waves. But it sure was an experience. It would have been an even better one for Dirk had I been more patient!

Next year my sister Hannelore and her girlfriend, Olli, both city-girls, were visited with us, and I suggested a five day canoe trip for the three of us. Up to the Boundary Waters we went and encountered lovely 100 degree temperatures. We slogged through it. On the second day I made my one and only orientation error ever in late afternoon and, taking a wrong portage, ended up at a dead-end little lake. On the portage we saw lots of bear poop which spooked the two women quite a bit. Pooped and sweaty, we decided to spend the night at the small lake, too tired to tackle the correct portage that evening. We all needed a bath. I said: I'm going to skinny-dip. It's up to you what you want to do. The two joined me as is. For the first time, I saw my sister in the nude, and from thenon was able to see and accept her as a woman, not my kid-sister! And did those ice-cold beers taste good after five days drinking "luke-cold" lake waters! We retired to an Ely restaurant and after a steak dinner, to the bar. In the course of this R'n'R afternoon, I imbibed seven 7&7s, Hannelore 8, and Olli 9. Too bad Olli later became an alcoholic.

Prior to the canoe trip I also took them on a trip to Georgian Bay in Lake Huron, Ontario. For three years I also ran the affairs of our Canadian sister company. Once back, Ute, Hannelore, Olli and I drove from Chicago out through Colorado, Utah, Arizona back home. It was the first time we saw the Grand Canyon.

It is kind of tedious to list all these trips and vacations. However, they appear to constitute something like anchor points in the course of life. Some of them, small and large, I don't even list here.

My recollection when all these excursions took place has become somewhat hazy, not from senility yet, but due to the multitude of events. And, be patient, reader, other kinds of stories are yet to come.

A few weeks later, we had talked the Morrisons, friends and neighbors on Cambourne Lane, into another canoe trip of 11 days. They too, had no experience in such a venture. Judy Morrison was concerned about how to shave her legs during the trip! Together with their three sons we set off towards Ely again. Temperatures were still in the low hundreds. It was a hot summer. We had four canoes, so that John and I had to traverse each portage twice, carrying about 70 pounds on our shoulders. The women and kids had to portage the backpacks, one of which alone held 21 loaves of bread! The evening of the second day we adults had had it and contemplated discontinuing the trip. We decided to give every participant a vote – and promptly were outvoted by the six children. Thus we continued. And having our friend John along, we couldn't even ask the children to let us know when they had to go to the ..... Throne. Johns had been set up by the park service at each campsite. One night, at a beautiful campsite with, however, only one good site, which we let the Morrisons have, I picked a passable one, a bit slanted, right beside a little bush trail, the entry to our 5-person tent facing west. I slept by the opening, then came Ute, with the children following towards the back of the tent. An unexpected midnight storm caused water to run down the little trail and into the tent, collecting towards the bottom end. The kids pulled in their air mattresses, sleeping bags and legs, but the waters kept rising. What was I to do to save my family from drowning? Ute's legs were also up. The solution was to stab a hole into the bottom end of the tent. While water was still coming in the front, it could now exit at the end. We had a creek going through our tent. For various other excitements and experiences, space for all these details is insufficient. All the above events took place in the mid-nineteen seventies.

255

An aside. John Morrison was for me the typical American male. Raised in the Kansas countryside, he had all the 'charm' of such an American, also some of the hang-ups. At times I loved to put my hand very casually on his knee while sitting next to and talking to him, to see him cringe inwardly – I think. One time I had told him, that I valued two human characteristics above all others – competence and good will. When I asked him some time later which of the two I would choose, if I had to, he answered 'Competence'. Well, John, my response was: "I would pick good will. While I value competence, I feel, that without good will I cannot have competence. But competence by itself can exist very well without good will."

For a couple of years in the latter seventies I also played racket ball with three other guys, one of whom was John Morrison. Towards the end of the two years I was able to occasionally beat the weakest of the three. I just never was an athlete. Playing against Ute I had a bit of a better chance – in racket ball.

In 1975 Ute and I made our first trip with Club Mediterranee to Tahiti, Bora Bora and Morea. Our friend, Audrey, came from Burlington, Ont., to Schaumburg to watch over our three. Sailing on the lagoon on Bora Bora and skin diving in the lagoon on Morea were unforgettable experiences. But dancing with some lascivious hags on Bora Bora, I did not, when called upon.

Then, in 1978 we went once more to Morea – with the children – to introduce them to these magical isles. But on the nude beaches, that each Club sported, they were uncomfortable.

In 1981 we had the first Rutkowsky family gathering in Jackson Hole, WY. Kirsten refused to come along. There were Alfred and Gertrud Rutkowsky, Dorothea R. with her then still significant other, Günter Klingebeil, Ute and I, Christa and Ernest Schubert, Michael and his first wife, Dirk and Karen, and, last but not least Sabine Sponer, daughter of Ute's cousin, Irmgard. She fell into our children's age bracket.

As things went, we had arranged with her mother, that she would stay with us for the duration of a year to improve her English. I was able to have her join a class at our local High School w/o charge. Shortly after she arrived, I had to do an extended business trip by car through Indiana, Ohio, Pennsylvania into Ontario, where I was also in charge of Kuhlmann Canada Ltd. at the time. On the way north we visited our old friends, the Harringtons in Ohio, then the Clarks in Burlington. We also took a trip farther north to Georgian Bay with its 10,000 islands, included a nice skinny-dip in a secluded little bay and, on the boat ride back, when Sabine tried out running the motorboat, had the scare of our lives when the prop hit an unseen underwater rock and got jerked out of the water. Had it wrecked the prop, it would have been a long time rowing back to the boat rental place.

I wanted to introduce Sabine to King Crab Legs at a restaurant in Oakville, Ontario, I had been to before. Entering the place, the owner, an ex-German, approached us. When I asked him: "Do you have crab legs?", he grinned, bent dow, pulled up one of his trouser legs and asked: "Do I have crab legs?" Don't ever say Germans, or rather ex-Germans, have no sense of humor.

Another stop at the Clarks in Burlington resulted in Sabine being invited to stay with them for a week. I do not recall how she returned to us in Schaumburg.

A second Rutkowsky family reunion took place in 1983, again in Jackson Hole. It was close to the parents 50s anniversary, so it was celebrated there. The question arose, what to do that very evening, how to celebrate it, to make it special. I suggested to ask the parents to recount their early experiences in life, particularly how they met, how they got to Indonesia, and the years until Gertrud Rutkowsky with her three children returned to Germany in 1947. Alfred Rutkowsky had already been freed in India and shipped home in 1946 from seven years of internment in Dehra Dun at the foothills of the Himalayas. It turned out a very interesting, lively and memorable account and evening.

Let me slip in here a bit of the Rutkowskys life story. At the beginning of WWII when Germany invaded Holland, the Dutch interned all Germans living then in Indonesia, a Dutch colony at the time. Women and children were kept in Indonesia, the men, like all Axis males, that is Germans, Austrians and Italians, were gathered in Dehra Dun at the foothills of the Himalayas. Then, when the Japanese conquered Indonesia, they 'liberated' the women and children of their Axis allies, Germans, etc. The poor Dutch had it worse now. Gertrud Rutkowsky now lived with her children in one of the former Dutch homes, but at first without any means of support. Finally, they were 'kind of liberated' once more by Allied forces and lived in some camps. The war in Asia against Japan came to an end only in September of 1945. But soon the Indonesians rose against their colonial masters. Once the transportation means existed, the Dutch were eager to get rid of foreigners and shipped them to their home countries. All in all, it took six weeks in the 'bottom' of a ship for the Rutkowskys to get to bombed out Germany. Ute, at 11 years of age, would have loved to turn around and go back to Sumatra.

And once more did we have a family reunion of the Rutkowsky adults, in this case we assembled in Murnau, Bavaria. We stayed in a large private house of many rooms. One evening, we were sitting together with our host, quaffing some beer he tapped himself, an elderly man came in, talked a few moments with our host – I think he picked up some beer, because stores were closed already – and left again. He clearly spoke perfect German, actually more the Bavarian dialect. When our host came back, he told us, that this man was actually an American, living in the community for many, many years.

13. Escapade majeure –
and getting into things!

Now, let's take a break from trips and travels, move a bit back in time, and return to business and related matters! Business, by that time was going quite well. My income had increased substantially and we had begun to make our first investments. And my sights were set already to accumulate sufficient wealth to be able to retire at age 55, which I also conveyed to my superiors at Kuhlmann in Germany. By then I had a new boss in Germany by the name of Heinz Lossie, the new managing director. And with him I did not see quite eye to eye.

Kuhlmann America Inc. also needed bookkeeping to be done. It was taken care of by a freelance accountant, Jim Oldson, who, eventually, turned the task over to his wife, Mimi, 29 years of age. There was always a transfer of documents going on and we got to know this couple also on a social basis. Eventually, when I was also put in charge of Kuhlmann Canada Ltd., after the remaining personnel up there had left or was terminated, I traveled by car to Oakville, Ontario, to assume this task and transfer information and accounting materials – together with Mimi Oldson. Twice in my life I had the experience, having met women: Keepa your hands off! This was one of the occasions. Yet, at the time, I felt very much a lack of being physically wanted! When the invitation came in Canada, I went for it – against my better knowledge. But I was hooked and the whole thing evolved into a drawn-out affair of many months. And all, or most of it, in the open. As it turned out, this couple operated in, what at the time was called, an "open marriage".

At forty-one I had arrived at my midlife-crisis – and it put our marriage on the rocks. Eventually, Ute and I decided to "take a break" in our relationship. With her sister Christa living in Long Beach, it was decided that she move there with the children, so we bought a house in Long Beach, and the four took off across the country to the West Coast.

I continued my affair(s) in Schaumburg, took another brief canoe trip in the Boundary Waters with the Oldsons, but also took a number of "redeye flights" to Long Beach. Finally – I / we had come close to separation – I had enough and asked Ute to come back. After about half a year she did.

I had gotten "the worst" out of my system, but not all. Some of my "sights" were changed forever by the afore experience. But, eventually, after a couple of more dalliances, I was able to settle down.

We rented out the house on Volk Ave., in Long Beach. By that time we had accumulated enough funds to purchase an additional house. Before all the above transpired, we had actually thought of purchasing a vacation home at one of the small lakes in upper Wisconsin. We had even found one, a log house with five bedrooms and a thousand feet of lake frontage – the broker would have bought 100 feet – all for $ 50,000 at the time. But we figured, if we buy it, we'll have to make use of it, that is, travel up there often, beating the Chicago traffic back and forth, all taking maybe 5-6 hours of driving each way. Our preference, however, was to see more of the world and rather spend money on foreign trips.

By that time I took out an equity line of credit on our Schaumburg house, at a time when this was not very popular yet. I financed two CNC machines, one new, one used, for one of my customers, whose bank would not extend the requisite loans to him. It was a bad time for small business in the late 70s, when banks were very skittish making loans to small companies. For the new machine, I first checked with the management in Germany, whether my plan was acceptable to them. Since it meant Kuhlmann could sell a pricey machine they readily agreed.

Within a year, after having rented out the Volk Ave. house, we purchased another one in Long Beach for rent. We had there as a contact the real estate agent, Bill Watilo, who also managed the properties. Often did we fly out to the L.A. area at the time. Sometimes it was for Kuhlmann business, sometimes for our own. Southern California had become a little bit like a second home to the Chicago area. And then we bought a third house, sight unseen, just having been looked at by my local Kuhlmann rep. I borrowed the moneys for the downpayment from the equity credit line, adding some savings, then paid the credit off as quickly as possible from surplus income and the rent income from the properties. It also made for nice tax deductions. It was unfortunate, that many years later, having trusted Watilo, he embezzled moneys from his clients' accounts and took us for about $4,000.

14. The Children.

Let's hop back once more to our arrival in Canada. When we boarded our Lufthansa flight in Frankfurt for Montreal via London, Dirk was 2-1/2 years old, Kirsten 1-1/2 years, and Karen in a carrying case, 5 months! Many, many flights later I learned to appreciate how well we crossed that ocean, our children making little fuss, compared to many others we later experienced.

We had had the best intentions for the children to maintain a knowledge of German. So we spoke German at home, figuring they would pick up enough English playing with other kids in the development. But, when Dirk, then Kirsten entered school, they turned out to be behind in English language development. We were asked by the teacher to use English at home, which we did. It did not take long and English had become the dominantly spoken language at home. We had a basement at this townhouse. One day, Dirk was playing in the basement, I heard the frequently shouted term: Bullshit, bullshit! I didn't use this term. So, where or who from had Dirk picked it up? A bit of contemplation had us arrive at Paul Harrington, our friend and neighbor. It was his favorite deprecative expression.

This, our basement, also had a window with a window well. One day, Ute found a small skunk facing her through that window. It had fallen in. How to get the critter out without getting skunked. She lowered a baited carton on a string with a little trapdoor down and – voila – the skunk entered. She closed the trap door with a stick and pulled the critter out, carried it to the adjacent woods that had remained and opened the trap door. A day later, the skunk was once again in the window well. It must have been the tasty bait Ute had used. How the second event was resolved, I do not recall. It is also immaterial. Most important was that Ute didn't get skunked and smelled.

One day Dirk had disappeared and Ute's frantic search located him at the nearby police station. He had been picked up wandering. The officers had given him chocolate which caused Ute great worries in that the four year old tike would take off again for more chocolate.

Please understand, that many of the events I recount here, are not in chronological order. It is the events that were retained, not the time frame as such.

Kirsten eventually needed glasses! She was behind in school, and only through her trouble in school did we find out her deficit. Many hours of vision training were subsequently required, but the problem was solved and she advanced. On one of our mini-vacations at Eels Lake in Ontario – we had driven up there from Chicago to meet with the Clarks – Kirsten, standing on a little boat dock, had lost her glasses in the murky, about five foot deep waters. I recall my repeated diving efforts, groping on the mucky bottom, to retrieve the precious object.

Oh, and when I arrived at this Eels Lake by bus – Ute and the kids had taken our car there – I walked in from the main road to the camping place, to be happily greeted by a strange woman. Only after closer inspection did I recognize Ute, who had been severely bitten by blackflies, her face now all swollen up. In the evening, sitting around a fire on camp chairs, we had to put mosquito coils underneath the chairs, so as not to be stung by the beasts through the chair's webbing. Once, making tea in the dark, we found about a hundred drowned bugs in the boiling water.

There was also a bet made with the Clarks which I never collected on. It was for a case of red wine. They maintained, that by the year 2000 – we were then in the mid-seventies – cars would no longer play a role in transportation. I ridiculed that proposal!

When the children were still young, I also tried to teach them German in regular sessions. They made good progress and I think my method worked well. However, as much too often I, at times, became impatient. And when I once slapped Dirk across the cheek, which left some finger marks, I recalled my dad's slaps on the back of my head, when I did not comprehend a mathematical problem. I decided to rather quit German lessons than have the children encounter more of this experience.

263

We never resolved to send the children on weekends to German lessons. First we could not afford it, and later it did not seem to be of importance to us. All had retained a passing knowledge of the language, some of it due to several visits with my parents in Germany. The four, that is including Ute, did their first return visit to Germany in 1969, five years after our arrival in Canada. This was about a week after Ute had flipped over our Nova automobile after having dropped me off at work in Oakville. She was hanging upside down in the seatbelts – with only a few scratches. It all happened at rather low speed in a curve. Oh, well!

One time, when Dirk returned solo from Germany, he arrived with all kinds of treasures from the plane. He had even been invited to the cockpit. But then he had plundered all the little soap bars from one of the toilets, postcards, etc. When Karen and Kirsten returned once alone, their seat neighbor was a Middle Eastern man. He wore one of these trick rings one can take apart. He offered the girls $10 if they could. Karen tried first, but gave up. Kirsten, with her greater patience, set to work and fiddled it apart. Was she proud to have accomplished it and to have made ten bucks in the process!

For all too many years the raising of the children was left to Ute. I was engaged in giving my various employment situations a go, also had to travel frequently. And while we did 'things' together, in retrospect I must say, that I was much too distant, and when I was not distant, I was too little involved – just as my dad had been with me. I do not mean this to be understood as an excuse, but as a matter of unfortunate fact. In later years, I have had to admit to various parties, when the subject came up: I have not been a good father!

Then Karen got into trouble. To resolve it I / we gave her two stark choices. She opted for one, but I think she held it against me for a long time. I still think the way it went was the best for her. Yet it may have caused her to fall into the 'trap' of becoming a born-again-Christian – at least for a while, which made her quite unbearable. But, eventually, she got over and out of it.

The kids went to our local Junior College, William Rainey Harper, in Palatine, more or less up the road, except that Karen was the first to leave the house to go to Warren Wilson College near Asheville, NC. Before that, she had taken a leave of absence from learning and had stayed with my father and sister in Biebrich for a year. There, she had worked at the local American PX, where she met a young warrant officer, to whom she became engaged. Upon his discharge he returned to North Carolina where his parents lived. Well, as it turned out, he wanted to boss her, which she couldn't take. So they went their separate ways.

Getting her BA at Warren Wilson, Karen had gone on to get her Master's in social work at Tulane in New Orleans. There she met Blake Brocato and married him. For the event Ute and I, together with our Morrison friends, flew down there. A bit later the young couple moved to Asheville, NC, where we visited a couple of times. Now it was Karen's turn to 'boss' her husband who, in my opinion, lacked drive. After a couple of years he wanted to go to seminary school – the two were very religious – and they moved to Jackson, Mississippi. There, Karen found out that things were not going well and, in a 'cry-for-help' made a suicide attempt, following which Ute flew down there. When Karen then wanted to part from Blake, she lost all support from their "Christian" friends, which seems to have been a profound lesson. Then they divorced.

Karen stayed on in Jackson for several years and finally gave me my first 'granddog' as she called it, Kiki, a miniature poodle. Then, through the mails, she made contact again with a former school mate from Warren Wilson, Paul Kissel, who had gone his own ways and had divorced from a failed marriage. He came from San Jose, CA, to visit Karen and they picked up from where they had left several years before. Since San Jose didn't afford them acceptable housing, they moved to Bend, OR, where they now have two daughters, Natalie and Emma. At the time I'm editing this account their marriage is on the rocks and they may very well separate.

Kirsten, after a couple of years at Harper, left for Northern Illinois University in DeKalb for a BA in Psych. When Kirsten was finished there, she first lived with us in Schaumburg, but needed to "get out of the house". After having worked for a time at a title insurance company, she eventually decided to also move to Tucson. There was a brother to fall back on!

Another title insurance provided work. Eventually, she went into massage training and made her living, kind of, in it. Both of us got involved in trying to get her out of a limited existence and in the process she went to ASU to get a masters in social work. Yet, when finished, she found it wasn't for her, and resumed work and training in massage therapy. Through the years she had gone through many boyfriends, that we sometimes "despaired" of her ever settling down. But then, lo and behold, she found Felipe Morales who seemed to "fit the bill"! They now live in their own house in Tucson.

Dirk puttered along at Harper, his grades being poor. Then we arranged, that he would have to pay himself for any course he concluded with a grade worse than C. When this didn't work either, we told him, it was time to look for something else to do. Maybe a year or so prior to his departure, I had the idea of having the south side of our house clad in aluminum siding. I offered Dirk the job, although he had never done something like this. He did a good job, eventually a second side, and finally the rest. These tasks, well executed, got him into the handyman business, with him finding little building projects and repairs in the neighborhood. So, when he left – he had decided on Tucson, AZ – he knew what he could do. It was only a matter of finding customers at the new place. It had been his intention to take courses at ASU, but those petered out in the next two years, as he became full-time engaged as a handyman. And handy, he was. Much later he performed numerous tasks repairing, remodeling and repainting our home in Prescott. But that was many years later!

Around 1994/95 he entered into a relationship with Teresa Wilke. The two lived together and, against his wishes, she got pregnant, then gave birth to a son, Moshe Paul – Wilke. Dirk did not give his family name to his son! While he has done an admirable job as a father, much much better than I ever did, this not giving him his name has at times pained me. I have tried to look at it two ways. One being an existential one tells me: What does a name matter! It's the human being that counts, and using the male's name is just a social custom. But then

– I know, that there's only one other Windolf line in Leimen near Heidelberg with only two daughters. It will be the end of this line of Windolfs. But consider: Had Johanna married, no longer would there have been the name Windolf. So, what does it all matter.

What matters is, that these days I can explore various matters Dirk or I bring up, trying to understand their implications. In these occasional conversations we do find each other.

I may have mentioned it someplace else in these scribblings, that one of the most important things I seem to have been able to pass on to the children was not to have ethnic prejudices. As a child I recall to have seen people on the street in Germany wearing a big yellow Star of David on their coats, identifying them as Jews. I have kept for years, and still do, a photo showing the selection of Jews arriving on the railroad ramp in Auschwitz, healthy ones who could work on one side, feeble ones, women and children to the other – for extermination, murder. To drive the point home, I imagined, had I been born differently, to have arrived at this very ramp with my family. Helpless to object, not knowing what was going to happen, but having a certain certainty, that things were going the wrong way. This is what I passed on to you, children! Continue doing so for generations to come! This is why I am retaining German citizenship, because I feel I cannot run away from what happened in the past – done by mu people.

15. Ute's Growth.

When my employment became very shaky in late 1971, we arrived at the conclusion – we never had any intentions of returning to Germany – to put ourselves on two legs, that is, two incomes. For this, Ute needed to acquire schooling for a profession. Her exposure to three nurses in Canada probably provided the idea for a like career. In 1971 she went to Harper College for a two-year associate degree in nursing. When finished in 1974, she went to work at Alexian Brothers Hospital in Elk Grove Village, about 8 miles away. One not so "springy" morning, driving to work – the studded tires had come off the day before due to legal requirements – a late snowstorm had hit. Then and there I got the call, that her car was hanging with its front over the guard rail guarding a small pond – or was it Ute? Since then she has been "good", except for a few scratches here and there. But such events I've always seen as 'minor things'! There are bigger "things" to worry about.

When my "escapade" was over and all had returned from Long Beach to Schaumburg, she wanted to continue her education, that is, acquire a BS in nursing, since the associate degree would have kept her always stuck in a lower nursing position. I had had a young woman, daughter of a former colleague of Ute, working for me as a bookkeeper for a while. When she left, Ute took this on as a part time position. It was hard to get into bookkeeping and some secretarial work, particularly working for or with me, her husband. But with a few tears it worked out very well, and she became my best office helper of all that I had.

This part time job enabled her to enter Northern Illinois University in DeKalb, about 50 miles one way from Schaumburg to study for her BS. And after many miles of driving back and forth, she made it – and good! Thus I needed another secretary/bookkeeper, whom I found in Barbara Wood, just two years my junior. By that time, business had grown, Barb came in full time and stayed with KAI for 10 years.

Ute then went to Parkside General Hospital in Park Ridge working in substance abuse for seven years. The terrible stories she brought home at the beginning, made even our one beer at dinner taste sinful, and for a while we even shared one (1) can or a bottle of beer.

When she had enough there, she moved to Northwest Community Hospital in Arlington Heights in psychiatric/geriatric care. And after two and one half years she was tired of this and quit. But then we were already in preparation for our move southward.

Nursing in Prescott paid very poorly, about half what she had earned in Chicago before quitting. She was very glad of not having to work and slid happily into retirement. Joining the Art Docents, having to study art, and to give a presentation of her study area kept her busy for some time. When she had completed her studies, she visited some school classes to carry art to children. But it did not suit her talents. So, she eventually settled in to prepare slides for aspiring Docents, that is for their talks. Being independent in this task suited her well.

And that brings us to photography. I had given up taking photos many years ago. More and more I had found, that I saw the world more through a view finder, than directly, real. But Ute had picked up photography, so we had someone in the family to take pictures of some of our many trips. Then Dirk built a darkroom in a basement spare room, and now Ute could really go after her desire, that is, taking close-ups of flowers, grasses, and other small things of the natural world. Many turned out very beautiful, and over time she has sold a number of images. She could sell even more, if she would be inclined to market herself, or rather her pictures. But her desires seem to go more into taking and developing these black and white images, than selling herself / them.

16. Going back to School.

Let me jump way ahead, even past the courses I have been teaching, to today, the 26th of December 2004. Today is the day, actually yesterday, when tens of thousands have died, have been injured, have lost relatives and friends and their earthly possessions in Southeast Asia from the magnitude 9.0 earthquake off the west coast of Sumatra. I've just done a tiny bit to help Doctors w/o Borders to assist in this dire situation. It is, will be the greatest natural disaster to strike humanity in our time – hopefully.

A couple of years ago, shortly after I gave my course: "Cataclysms and Extinctions", I did warn of complacency and even bigger calamities that WILL strike us. Then, I did also write a verse, expressing my concerns. So, here it goes. It's not that hot and by far, does not list all that may happen. I didn't even mention a big earthquake, but... The Universe is a violent place:

With Ute getting an education at college, I felt kind of left behind. So I thought to give it also a try. It must have been 1978 that I applied at Harper College, up the road, and the "dropped-out" was accepted without any question. I even tested out in English, without ever taking another class in Canada or the US. But this is also why I have retained all this German grammar infecting my writings in English. It isn't word power, it's this Teutonic grammar! But, so what!

Now I began to juggle business with school. As much as possible I took evening classes. This worked very well and I do not think that business suffered. For a couple of German courses I was able to test out. When it came to two higher level ones, I had to take them, but was transformed into a kind of teaching assistant. They were all easy credit, though.

My instructor in a couple of anthropology courses was Saul Sherter. He endeared himself to me when, during one of his courses, a young woman up front in some context declared herself to be an agnostic. Sherter shot back: Ah, a chicken-atheist. But he was a good man. After the course a few students, including myself, usually gathered with him to continue discussing whatever subjects remained. I

270

recall a day when, in this group, I became involved in an intense exchange with a woman about my age. When the group drifted apart, the two of us sat outside in the sun, continuing our exploration which involved a problem of hers its subject I no longer recall. As it progressed, I sensed that she was unwilling or unable to open up more and we discontinued our conversation. We parted and I never knew her name. What was so exceptional in the course of this exchange was the enormous clarity, the lucidness of my mind that had evolved. I never before and never again felt so clear, elevated and understanding at this brief time, knowing already, that my mind would settle back into its normal, comparatively dull existence!

Taking a class in geology, my instructor was Paul Sipiera, eleven years my junior. It turned out, that he was intent on marrying during this class and, as it happened, his fiancee walked out on him two weeks before the wedding. He was devastated! I, being an exceptional student – I'm referring to my age then – had become friendly with Paul. And when he needed an ear to discharge his sorrow, we became friends. This friendship and mutual admiration has lasted to today. I still think Paul is the best instructor I have ever come across.

He has an enormous talent to get into all kinds of things and meet all kinds of people. The latter include a variety of Apollo and Shuttle astronauts, some of whom I had the good fortune to meet. They were all highly interesting, educated and alive people. Paul's ventures include five trips to Antarctica, all for the collection of meteorites. He founded the Planetary Studies Foundation for the study of meteorites and the dissemination of science to the public, of which I have become a member. Some little science and travel articles I've written have appeared or will appear in his quarterly periodical.

Paul Sipiera acquired his Ph.D. in 2004, after many years of trying, from the University of Innsbruck, based on his lifetime accomplishment, about 160 scientific articles. Just before that, in 2004, I traveled up to Chicago for one of his benefit dinners, where about 250 people of all stripes had gathered, the keynote speaker being the former Apollo astronaut, Dr. Edgar Mitchell. He conveyed, among other things, the epiphany he experienced leaving the Moon and seeing the Earth suspended in space. The three of us breakfasted together.

Then Paul Comba asked me whether I could extend a landscaping job I had done around his observatory years ago. When I started he asked me to send him a bill when finished. I suddenly had the bright idea to fulfill my other friend, Paul Sipiera, a deeply desired wish. I asked Paul Comba: "Forget the invoice. Would you, please, name one of your many, as yet unnamed asteroid discoveries for Paul Sipiera. And that he did. Now there's also a 'Sipiera' asteroid out there in the asteroid belt, with the number 31,931, an absolute magnitude of 15.4, and a diameter of between 2 to 5 km.

Some time in the early 80s Karen traveled with him to Italy, while Ute and I cruised farther north, eventually meeting in Bern, Switzerland. There, Paul presented a paper at a scientific meeting. From Bern, Ute and I drove into the country north of Bern to track down a farm where she had stayed in 1948 and 1949, following her arrival in Germany from Indonesia to get better nutrition and to improve her health. The experience had remained vivid in her memory. When we finally found it and drove into the yard, there stood a farmer with a young girl holding a horse. Ute approached and said: "I'm Ute..." And the man completed the sentence with:"... Rutkowsky", her maiden name. She must have left quite an impression for him to remember the name after more than 30 years! We were well received for an impromptu afternoon coffee and cake. Following this, the four of us traveled through the Alsace back to Frankfurt.

In another year, or was it after Bern, Ute, Paul and my sister accompanied me to Bad Lauterberg in the Harz Mountains. I had to conduct some business with Kuhlmann and, Bruno Schönborn, superb host as always, took us all out for an extensive dinner and subsequent drinks at his home. Around midnight we were promenading through Lauterberg's Kurpark along the Lutter Creek. There we saw concrete stairs with a railing leading into the shallow waters. One could "kneip" in there. Paul, Ute and Hannelore all took off their footwear, socks, etc. and descended into the waters, afterwards goose-stepping through the grass to dry off again. Bruno and I slept well that night, the other three miserably or not at all. "Kneiping" in cold water stimulates circulation, ergo...

My worst grade at Harper was a C. It was in chemistry. I had to take the final test for this class some time in January (it was a Fall 2 class), because my mother had suddenly died two weeks before Christmas. It had been my intention to fly over there for Christmas and New Year, to hear on Sylvester once more the midnight racket of firecrackers going off, church bells ringing, and ships on the Rhine tooting their horns. But I had to fly earlier now. In the past, upon my arrival 'at home', my mother had always brought out one or two cold minis of Sekt, sparkling wine, to welcome me. That had come to an end now.

When I had finished at Harper I transferred to Northern Illinois University – remember, that was a drive of 50 miles one way. Again, I took evening or extension courses, but that was not always possible. I enjoyed being with younger people, being an old fart among them, but that gave me a bit of a special status. While there were some middle-aged women, having gone back to school once their children had come of age, a male of my age was rare to find at university. I had latched on to a few of these "elderly" females and, at times, a few of us gathered at a nearby cafe to hash things over. As it turned out, one of them would have loved to snatch me. Often, my fellow-students criticized an instructor for his or her shortcomings. I rarely did. I had found, that it was more important to focus on what an instructor was able to give. Where's the value?! That was what counted for me.

Since I had to take courses whichever way I could at Northern, that is that they would not interfere with my business activities, I sometimes took Independent Studies, particularly when I expected business travels during a semester. Once I did this with an anthro instructor, an Afghani. It was more or less a one-on-one relationship. I told him about my strong bias to Islam and discussed it widely with him. I think I can say, that in our general discussions and exchanges about anthropology, he was the instructor who challenged me most intellectually. But I think I gave back too. He had a brother married in Germany to a German woman. So, while I visited Germany during the semester, I called this brother and had the longest chat with him and his wife. Back in the US, I invited my instructor with his wife and teen son for dinner – 50 miles distant, remember. As it happened his brother from Germany was then visiting. So I told him: "Bring him along". It was cute. There was the 'German' Afghani in suit and tie sitting very upright, and the American Afghani in pullover, sitting relaxed at the table. Ute had prepared a lamb dish. For dinner the Germanized and Americanized Afghanis had a beer. When I mentioned Ratzeputz, a German 126 proof digestive, which I had at home at the time. The German Afghani knew it. Now the American Afghani had to try it too, after he heard how awful it was.

At Harper I had become sidetracked from my interest and study area of anthropology by my friend Paul. I took several geology and astronomy classes with him. At NIU, I now concentrated more on anthro, but took a few courses in psych. Oddly, though, although I've always been interested in the subject, I was only able to make Bs, never an A. I believe it was 1982, that I took part in an archeological dig on the Mogollon Rim in Arizona. It was a large enterprise, where students from various universities in the country participated in. The first evening after the NIU people's arrival, the chief scientist took us on a walk across the area to be explored. Actually, he took us up a hill with lots of overgrown pits. These, he explained, had been grave sites, excavated by grave robbers looking for precious ceramics. Here and there, one could find small bones of the once-interned. Coming to a maybe 10 ft by 30 ft long rock assemblage, seemingly the outline of an old stone structure, he asked us what we thought it might have been. I was very cautious, since some rocks were aligned diagonally. No one hit onto the right idea. He explained: When cross-country flights began in the early twenties, navigation was still haphazard. Aircraft flying east from Los Angeles needed to refuel at Winslow, AZ. So, there, on a bare hillock, a little west of Winslow, lay once the rock outlines reading: WINSLOW, pointing in the direction of the town. This stay is a story in itself, told many times, but too long to hold down here.

In the spring of 1985 in graduated with a BA. I had taken two physical anthro courses as the last two before graduation. My instructor then was a fellow graduate of Tim White's, one of the foremost anthropologists in the US of our time. I had the good fortune to be introduced to him. When, after a farewell party in DeKalb, I drove my instructor home, he asked me at the door: "Herb, what are you going to do now?" My answer was: "I have to make a decision between going on for a Master's, or to become financially independent." I did choose the latter! But I was also a bit concerned of the math tests I would have to pass to get into a Master's program. Anyway, I was always good in arithmetic, smaller fry. I could calculate profits! But now I could also pass muster with my "educated" wife.

17. Contemplations.

I believe two factors, more than any others, have influenced my life and impacted also Ute and the children! And both factors are intimately related. Had I had the wherewithal for a "normal" successful education, my life, I think, might also have followed a somewhat different, more "normal" route. But I failed at this early in my life. Yet parallel to this failure I was exposed to the covert and overt admonitions and expectations of my paternal grandmother and parents to accomplish something – whatever – to get ahead.

It is my interpretation, that these pushes and pulls caused me to "go for it" after all, once I had woken up. Yet, then, I had to do it education-wise from a much lower base. To succeed from where I was in my mid-teens, I now had to demand a lot of myself. And the search began. My impatience is likely connected with this "striving", with all its positive and negative consequences. Thus the need to succeed came also at a cost, for my demands extended also to Ute and the children! All of them have the urge to either be or become good at what they are doing! Not that I want to claim all the credit, though.

In 1985, only a few months after I had graduated from college, my father died. Both my parents were gone. 'Only' my sister Hannelore remained of the immediate family. I was the oldest. I had achieved financial security, had become a millionaire. I had quite successfully represented a German company in the United States – was still doing it. And I had received a BA from a university. In a way I had accomplished, in my opinion – it had never specifically been talked about – all the 'things' my parents had wanted for me as a boy. And now a deep depression enveloped me, lasting about two years.

This 'desire' of my family to better myself had always been implicit. And now, that I had done it – what else was there to do. Ute wanted me to see a psychiatrist, take medication, but I refused. The thought of taking my life never occurred to me at the time. Way inside I knew I would get out of this in time. And I did.

Later on, too, did I have to deal with bouts of depression, sometimes lasting only a day or two, sometimes weeks or months. At times, I could feel one coming on, as if a chemical imbalance was striking me, only to fade within a few days. If I learned one thing – and

276

just these days I came across it again – if I'm in the dumps, if something has failed me, or if I have failed myself – I shall overcome! I have done it many a times, and with luck and perseverance shall do so in the future. But then, I've never put much stock into luck. Luck is largely what we make it to be. This is also why I rarely wish other people luck. No – I wish them success!

What also crystalized during the years is my belief in finding solutions. Solutions to whatever problems arise. Not that solutions come out of the blue sky, no, they usually evolve in a process. And solutions often require compromise. Hey, what's wrong with compromise. I still can remain true to myself!

Two other capabilities became important to me. The first was/ is the furthering of awareness, awareness of my surroundings, what's nowadays called 'situational awareness', I did call in the past 'environmental awareness'. This includes the physical world as well as the world of empathy, fathoming, among other things, the impact one has on others feelings or others feelings per se.

And then there was the call for 'autonomy', that I, Ute, the children, and others ought to be able to take care of themselves, and that this trait should be supported whenever possible. In a marriage, once autonomy is achieved, nothing then prevents an arrangement delegating those tasks better executed by one partner to the other.

I have had no 'heroes' in my life. But there are two, maybe three people, I admire. They are Sir Ernest Shackleton (I was introduced to by Paul Sipiera), and Lewis and Clark. What do these people have in common? Well, aside from bringing back scientific and geographic knowledge, I admire them for having brought all their men (and one woman) back to civilization! If Meriwether Lewis and William Clark lost one man – from appendicitis – he would, at the time, have also died in New York City. These leaders took care of their charges!

I have also been a skeptic for most of my life. That must have started in my teens when I quit the Lutheran Church. This has not prevented me from taking in those ideas and facts I found reasonable,

277

just as I have been prepared to dump also those ideas that did not hold water.

And way back in the seventies I took on my first 'foster child' through a nonsectarian organization nowadays called Childreach. Since I had, and still have, this bias against Islam, I requested a Moslem girl in the Sudan. As I learned, it is better to support girls who, when they grow up and have children, are then better equipped to pass on to their offspring that which they have learned themselves. Men, in many cultures, are peripheral to the raising of children. My connection with this girl ended only when she was released from the program, that is, had arrived at womanhood in her country.

Then I had a boy (after all) in Equador for a number of years. Then a girl in Sri Lanka. By that time I had realized, that I was very poor in writing little exchange letters to these children. I felt bad. Then, the girl in Sri Lanka also graduated from the program. Due to my perceived inability to write these letters, but more so because of my retirement, I advised Childreach that I could not enter into new commitments. Yet, once secure in Prescott, I took on a girl in Tanzania, only to discontinue it with great regret. I just couldn't write these little letters. I cannot truly relate with small children, couldn't with mine, couldn't with others. Still can't! But for years now Childreach has authority to charge my Visa account every year the equivalent of a year's contribution, applying it to their general fund.

When we traveled in Sumatra we saw this multitude of children. Children, children everywhere! This is, when my views on supporting children changed. I discontinued my support of UNICEF and, for a while, that of Childreach. Not that it is also important, but why not go to the source to better the lives of children, prevent too many to be born, to then all too often live in misery and depravation. Thus, my favorite charity became a doctors' organization, nowadays called Engender Health, promoting voluntary contraception in many countries. And again, not to be bogged down with too many children, this empowers women. Worldwide, we've got to raise the status and the education of women to better all-round conditions.

And since I've cherished nature, my support for many years has gone to the Nature Conservancy, who does work with landowners, industry, and whoever, to accomplish its goal of protecting the shrinking diversity of life on the planet. Solutions are its goal!

And a final thought that has often crossed my mind. What if I had married someone else, one of my girlfriends of my early twenties? Where would I have ended up? Would I be divorced? What children would I have had? What might I have accomplished or failed at? Idle thoughts, but.... As my friend, Hans Möhlmann in Germany not too long ago did tell me over the phone – we call each other about every week or so – he who has a high and dear opinion of Ute, even put her in his will: "What you two accomplished, you did together". Amen and Hallelujah!

18. More Travels.

In the early 80s I felt the need to do something together with my father, to maybe find a bit of closeness I had missed all my life. When he came for a visit, my mother was already dead several years, I suggested a drive down Big Sur. We flew to San Francisco, drove up to Muir Woods to show him the Redwoods, then down towards Big Sur. However, winter storms had washed out part of the northern road and we had to drive partially through the interior to get to the coast. It was a good trip.

Four weeks after returning home from the Mogollon dig, Ute and I set off again for Arizona. This time it was for an eleven day rafting trip down the Colorado through the Grand Canyon. Before we got to Flagstaff, our jump-off point, I took Ute out into the "Wilderness", where we had looked for Indian artifacts. I had chosen to travel in two-oar-powered 15 ft rubber rafts. We were about 25 clients and 6 guides, of which two were women. It became an exhilarating trip with lots of screams passing the rapids. We entered at Lee's Ferry and got out at Diamond Peak. Once we had passed the Little Colorado River where upstream rains had fallen, the Colorado got very muddy. Arriving at a camping site in the evening, my first objective was always to find a good camp site, then a creek or a rainwater-filled basin to wash up in. Ute and I passed Lava Falls, the biggest rapids, in separate rafts, I with a woman-guide. Below, a couple of small somewhat sulfur-smelling streamlets dropped into the Colorado from a maybe 6 ft high embankment. Our bikini-clad guide asked her three charges whether it would be okay if she stripped to the buff and get a wash-off from the cleaner waters tumbling in. I got the honor to douse her with one of the bailing buckets. Ute's less pleasant experience was, that in one of the rapids a spare oak came loose and hit her upper right arm. She obtained an about 8" long bruise from it. Otherwise, we never had an emergency or accident on this trip.

Some time in the mid-eighties Ute, Dirk and I once more headed for Ely, Minnesota. Our outfitter there had arranged for us to fly into Quetico National Park in Canada, from where we were to canoe back to Ely. On one of the islands we camped we hit it right smack at blueberry time. We ate them for breakfast, lunch and dinner, together with plenty of fish Dirk caught. The outfitter's wife had given us two pepper containers instead of one salt and one pepper. Ute, ever inventive, spiced our fish, etc. with the concentrated soup mixes we had along.

It may have been next year, that we did a similar fly-in canoe trip to Quetico, Ute, I, Warner & Audrey Clark. For two days, we camped on a nice little island. One late afternoon we played strip-hearts, not poker. The game went well for me, and still fully clothed, I decided to get rid of my uncomfortable shoes and socks sitting cross-legged in the grass. And wouldn't you believe it, the challenge I had produced. Shortly thereafter, I was the first to sit in the buff. Audrey and I tried to enrich our diet with some fresh fish. Upon our return, with not a single fish caught and me totally frustrated, the other two were just rising from a skinny-dip in the waters. Crossing one of the many portages, I was first with a canoe. When I came to an about 12 meter long swampy area, which had to be crossed balancing on one relatively solid linear log assembly with a parallel flimsy one, I managed it safely and was waiting at the close-by next lake shore, when I heard a tremendous crash and cursing emanating from the woods. Not long after, Warner showed up carrying the second canoe, both muddy from top to bottom and front to end. One of the "flimsy" logs had given way, toppling him into the muck. Thus were the pleasures of canoeing. Yet they are among one of my very best travel memories.

Once Ute and I had reach 50 years, we found that the portaging had become too much for us. Our backs did hurt for a while after each trip. But then, we also did practically nothing to stay in shape during the rest of the year. The follies of "youth" we were still beholden to.

During the eighties Ute and I vacationed also for a week on St. Kitts in the Caribbean. Another trip took us to the big island of Hawaii and to Kauai, where we stayed on the rugged north coast. We hiked part of the Na Pali trail. Leaving our condo early, we eventually took a side trail inland following a creek. Toward its end we came to a 6 meter circular rock basin the creek was passing through. We stripped to the buff to clean up from the humid, muddy trail experience and had just dried and dressed up again when the first 'tourists' arrived. Taking a cruise in a Zodiak along the Na Pali coast, I recall the beautiful sight of giant turtles floating in the water. A try of poi did not require a repeat!

For another trip my sister Hannelore had flown in from Germany and Warner Clark from Toronto, now separated or already divorced. We met in Seattle, rented a car and 'circumnavigating' the Olympic peninsula, drove down the west coast to L.A., from where we returned to our points of origin.

For two years I had taken care of the affairs of my friend Paul Sipiera while he studied at the University of Otago in Dunedin, New Zealand. He expressed his thanks by giving me a free first class ticket with Continental Airlines from Chicago to Sidney, Australia. Through his many flights, he had accumulated sufficient mileage for this generosity. Now, while he had flown back to NZ, I rented a car in Sidney and drove up the east coast of Australia to Townsville. A side trip into a nature preserve and a hike in there, resulted in me coming out infested with six tiny leeches attached to my lower legs, some inside my runners. The bleeding took a day to finally stop. I took a few excursions, one, a five day sailing trip with six others in the Whitsunday Islands, a few days at a resort on Odysseus Island, and from there a flight to the barrier reef. Being a single traveler at the resort I was invited one evening by an elderly couple to join them for dinner. The gentleman looked like he might have been working in some vineyards in his earlier life. Both were very amicable. For an after-dinner drink they invited me for a tawny port, which I enjoyed very much. When, next evening after dinner I ordered one myself from the bartender, I learned that this very port came from the winery of the Australian couple I had had dinner with the night before.

Back in Townsville, I entered a store of Aussie memorabilia. A native Australian woman approached me, the only client, to help. And we got into quite a conversation about aboriginal lore. When I picked the 'crocodile' painting, she complimented me on my choice, since I hadn't fallen for tourist knickknack. It took two months to arrive in Chicago.

Then I stopped in another store for a couple of small mineral souvenirs to take home. Looking in one of the display cases, I saw, for my first time, a fire opal – and was enthralled. The sales lady offered to take it out for me to hold. And thus I was caught. That beautiful little fire opal cost about as much as my entire land trip. For our 25th wedding anniversary I had it set in a gold pendant with a chain. It is a great pity for me that Ute barely ever wears it, for unknown reasons!

On the flight home, Paul and I met in Auckland and then made a few days stop-over on the Big Island of Hawaii. I got to see the bay where Captain Cook was murdered and feed the Jacks in the water off our excursion boat. Holding the bread balled up in one hand, feeding with the other, these aggressive, about one and one half foot long fish soon discovered the reserve bread and went for it. It was as if small sharks had taken a liking to me and I quickly relinquished the bread.

Then Africa was calling again and we booked a trip to Kenya and Tanzania. It was a bit too early in the year, March, or the rains were late. We encountered a lot of mud and never saw the peak of Kilimanjaro due to clouds. There were three other women in our group. At Amboseli Lodge Vervet monkeys displayed their 'naughty' behavior. Quickly, one of these females, of the human ones, had come up with the ditty: "Herbert, the pervert Vervet". Sure, after a few days, I felt like one of the gals! I had purchased a small video camera for this venture and, having edited a two hour presentation of our adventures, later on did put quite a number of friends to sleep. In the Masai Mara we took a balloon ride in one of the largest hot air balloons in service. Dipping at one time down almost to the water level of the Mara River, we chased a herd of hippos along. The full-course breakfast after landing in the middle of nowhere, prepared on one of the balloon burners, was excellent. All in all, it was a fantastic experience. I finally had made it to the wilds of Africa that had been denied me in 1956. Our return trip, getting out of bed at the camp on the Mara, via Nairobi, Frankfurt, New York and a stopover in Cleveland, to Chicago, there getting into bed, took us 50 hours! Yes, there had been a late snow storm again in Chicago.

Our driver-guide in Tanzania had been a young, amicable 'Christian' man (Tanzania's population is part Christian, part Moslem),

Nikodemus Vallalarta. He was married and had three children, his family living in Arusha, while he took his tourist-charges on week-long trips around the country. He had mentioned to one of our women that he would love to get into farming, an occupation he had grown up in with his parental family. At the time of our visit Tanzania was just getting out of years of socialistic experiments, 'fashionable' at the time in Africa, under it's otherwise honorable leader, Nyere. Land could not be held in ownership but under lease only.

In Arusha, our guide Niko, as he was called, took us to an Indian-owned store of wood carvings and other tourist memorablia. Among all the shiny, polished ebony carvings Ute discovered in a corner the unpolished figure of an African scribe and man-of-letters carrying a book on his head, a disciple at his feet. And we quickly purchased this unique carving, charging it to my American Express credit card. We arranged to have it shipped, since it was too big for our suitcases.

On the drive from Arusha to the Kenyan border, I sat with Niko up front and quizzed him about his farming wishes. Following this, I promised to help him realize his dream by sending him a check for $700, enough to get him going. I also promised him help for the future. When we parted at the border, we fell into this elaborate black greeting ritual of shaking hands. Although I had never done this before, it just "flowed". And I felt very honored to have been accepted by a man of such different culture.

We stayed in touch by letter. The check took a couple of months to cash! Then he moved his family to southern Tanzania where land could be leased. He, himself, kept chauffeuring tourists, which guaranteed a secure income. I checked with ex-president Carter's Institute in Atlanta to, perhaps, get him access to fertilizer, an irrigation pump. His wife had to hire helpers to tend the field. Then pests struck. And no man was about to take charge of the problem. Only with 'ownership' is full engagement in a venture assured! The project failed and we, eventually, lost contact.

Before this happened, our statue, purchased with shipping prepaid, hadn't arrived for several months. I wrote to Niko to check with the store. He did, and found it sitting in a corner of the shipping room, packed it himself and had the store get it on the way.

To slip something in here. The Kenia-Tanzania trip we flew with Panam New York to Frankfurt – six weeks after Panam 101 was blown up over Scotland. Several years later, vacationing on Hawaii, we flew Aloha Airlines, two weeks after they lost part of the fuselage together with a stewardess. And when we later flew to Indonesia with United, having booked an upgrade to business class, we wondered why no one sat on the right side. Then it occurred to me: A few weeks before, the improperly secured cargo door on this side had blown open in a flight, ripping open the plane's fuselage and sucking out seats together with several passengers. The aircraft had landed safely! But we decided to also move to the port side.

In the late 80s the thought arose of visiting Ute's birthplace, Sumatra. I had suggested doing this, to fill a need I perceived to exist in Ute. Then, communication with her sister, Dörthe, in Berlin, and her partner of many years, Günter Klingebeil, resulted in plans to travel together. In the late 50s, early 60s, Dörthe had spent a number of years in Sumatra again, when her parents had returned there, her father teaching comparative religion, mainly Islam vs the Old Testament, at the local Batak university. Dörthe took Bahasa Indonesia lessons in Berlin to brush up on her language skills as our translator. Then, one party flying in from Berlin, the other from Chicago, we met in Singapore and flew to Medan on Sumatra. One of Vati's, Alfred Rutkowsky's former students, had become the dean of the university. We visited there and were also invited to their home for breakfast, nasi goreng, of course.

Our first overnight stay was in a nice motel in Pematang Siantar, which had once belonged to friends of Alfred and Gertrud Rutkowsky. Now it was in the hands of locals. Venturing out for the first time, the women had to buy a Durian, a large, football-size green bumpy-skinned tree fruit. Its chambered inside holds several golfball-size pits imbedded in a white creamy fruit flesh. The locals cut the 'football' open for the customer, if so desired, after which one can suck the fruit flesh off the pits. Well, what needs to be said is, that there are only two types of people, those who love to eat Durian, and those who find them abominable. They stink like a rotten corpse. Now, what do you think of people who love'm?! Valiantly, I ate some, but then burped

285

'rotten corpse' the remainder of the afternoon. Never again! The other three continued enjoying this delicacy whenever an opportunity offered itself. I, though, whenever spotting a pile of Durian vendors had piled up four to five foot high, took a very deep breath, held it, increased my approach speed, and exhaled only after a safe distance. The vendors only smiled knowingly.

We hired a driver with his van and took off, visiting the places Ute recalled from her childhood. Tears were flowing when she stood in front of the house they had lived in after the Japanese had 'liberated' them from the internment camp the Dutch had put them in, after Germany's start of the war.

During the Chinese New Year we stayed at a fancy hotel dating from Dutch colonial times, consisting of several low-slung buildings. That evening it seemed that all the Chinese from Medan had congregated there to celebrate the Chinese New Year. None went to bed. It was noisy as hell, people talking and radios blaring through the night. About 5 in the morning, Dörthe had wandered from their unit to ours talking with Ute, telling her that Günter wanted to leave – right now. What am I going to do? Ute gave her two Benadryl to give to Günter to get him to sleep. Next morning, Ute asked her: "Did it work?" "No", said Dörthe. "I took them. I slept." I had resorted to another old trick I had once applied staying at a California motel. Adjacent walls are electrically wired together, as I had learned at the engineering offices of Dorsch Gehrmann many, many years ago. Our Chinese friends next door were the noisiest. So I pulled the plug of a lamp partially out and placed my knife blade across, intending to short out the lights and all else in their room. Would you believe it – ALL the lights, everything went dead across the entire compound – except, as Ute told me later, not the quackquackquack, not even for a minute! Alas, the hotel complex had a circuit breaker and everything was back to normal within a few minutes. Everything!

And we were scheduled to climb a dormant volcano next morning. On the way up through trees, passing small huts, we saw a water buffalo lightly tethered to a stake in the ground. I thought to demonstrate to city boy Günter, cautious even with dogs, that there was nothing to be afraid of. I approached the beast to pet it. I made it to within a couple of meters when the subdued snorting became louder and I figured retreat would be advisable. Better to lose my macho image than... When we prepared to go on, a little naked boy of maybe five years of age came out from the bushes, pulled the stake from the ground and led the big beast away. Sure, the critter knew the kid, but not me.

Higher and higher we ascended. Eventually the trail consisted of steep concrete steps dating back to Dutch colonial times. Above the tree line we found Indonesian laborers repairing old steps and building new ones. However, the material or the mixture they used did not hold up at all and the steps crumbled almost as fast as they built them. Maybe it was also the volcanic sulfur in the local sand they used. A story told by Ute's mother was, that when she and some friends climbed these very same stairs in the late 1950s, they were accosted by several Indonesian gun-toting youths. Ute's mother, fluent in Batak, reproached the crooks in a rush of words, among others: "What are your ancestors going to think of you" – this being a people revering ancestors – that they quickly disappeared. Sulfuric steam was emitted from several openings in the caldera. Indonesians had put burlap sacks over the openings to trap the sulfur. Ute wanted to take some pictures of one of the smaller open holes. It later turned out, that metal parts of her camera had been slightly corroded by the sulfur vapor. On our descent down the other face we encountered a viscous mud, not very deep, maybe only 2 - 4 centimeters, but immensely slippery. Ute slipped and got quite muddy. Soon we passed between straight-growing bushes and I cut four walking sticks which greatly facilitated our now three-legged descent.

We had paid our driver-owner every evening. One evening I did not have exact moneys. So I asked Ute to pay him. Next morning he did not show up, had abandoned us. We could only explain it, that he had been slighted being paid by a woman. He was a Moslem.

Who needed him. We made our way to Lake Toba, the largest wet-caldera in the world, with a size of about 100 by 25 km, with Samosir Island in the middle. There we stayed for a few days in a nice resort.

In Tarutung, Ute's birthplace, we could still see some of the trees planted by her grandfather, Herrman Weissenbruch, lining the village street. In Balige, near Lake Toba, Michael's birthplace, Ute's brother, we got to see a neat little church built by Ute's grandfather, which must have been around 1910. In the entrance hall stood two commemorative stones, one bearing the name of the mission's founder, Nommensen, the other grandfather's name Weissenbruch.

A story passed on by him to subsequent generations was, that when he arrived in Tarutung in 1906, an old Batak of the local tribespeople, of which there are nowadays about six million converted to Lutheranism, told him, that the 'Maus', the oval base of the thumb, was the most powerful, the tastiest part of a man. They had been cannibals. In fact the first two Scottish missionaries arriving in the area in the mid 19th century were supposedly eaten.

In another outlying village, Sitorang, our arrival was greeted by a throng of children, also some adults. One of the men, when told by Dörthe, that her grandfather had once lived here, offered to guide us around. He quickly conveyed to Dörthe, that his grandfather had provided the land for her grandfather to build his house. Nothing at all of it could be seen any longer, just some trees and bushes. Our visit must have been the entertainment of the day, if not the week or month, for these people.

As a souvenir I wanted to purchase an Indonesian sword. I did find one, bought it, figuring it would fit diagonally into my suitcase. Well, it did not. With the handle of my suitcase having been mauled, I decided to purchase a bigger suitcase in Medan. There, in a huge shopping center, which could have passed muster in any Western city, I found one. At the checkout counter stood three (3) young Chinese women, none speaking English. (Keep in mind, please, that there are millions of Chinese living in Indonesia) But then one of them established, that the suitcase bought had a numerical and a key lock, with the key missing. So we smiled at each other, while one went back to the luggage department to speak to the manager. Suddenly, I felt a small tuft of hair being pulled at my left arm. Turning, I looked at the smiling face of a maybe sixteen year old Chinese girl, still holding and pulling my arm hair. Knowing that Asians have little if any body hair, I knew what this was all about, and that she had to check this novelty.

288

She let go and I turned, since the manager with the key had arrived. But then my hair was pulled once more and turning, I found that her girlfriend had to give it a try too.

From Medan we flew to Bali, where we stayed in a beautiful guest house run by a young Balinese couple. While at the guest house, we were only wearing sarongs. Some older women in the countryside were still wearing only sarongs together with a slendang, a narrow 25 cm wide, two meter long colorful cloth, slung over one shoulder. Our young Balinese host told us, that younger Balinese looked askance at this habit. When he took us on a trip to a seaside resort where our three went swimming. He and I were rather having a cold drink at the open-air restaurant, when a Western female tourist came out of a cabin, flopped herself onto a lounge for sunning and took off her Bikini top. I asked him: "What about that?" His response: "She can do it. She's Western. She's not one of us!"

There's the story, that when the Dutch rather late conquered Bali in 1908, the royal Dutch couple came to visit. The governor asked the local chieftains along the road the royal couple was to travel to take care that the women lining the road were to cover their breasts. All was fine, except... as soon as the royal carriage approached, the women lifted their sarongs up over their breasts. A fine display of defiance!

Ubud and the surrounding villages, many specializing in different crafts, were a delight to shop. Often, Ute and I, having like tastes, snatched an appealing piece before Dörthe and Günter, who 'squabbled' too often: 'should we, should we not', were able to decide.

On our overnight return in Singapore I tried to find Tony Soon Ho in the telephone book, but failed. Then a phone message from Karen reached us. Hannelore had been diagnosed with lung cancer. I tried to find passage from Singapore to Frankfurt, but had no luck. So I decided to visit her via Chicago. It took us 30 hours for the return flight, in part because Chicago O'Hare airport was closed due to a snow storm.

19. Professional Changes and Accomplishments

As mentioned before, I had told management in the mid seventies, that I intended to 'retire' at age 55. After several failed attempts with other people, I succeeded to have Horst Zickermann, eleven years my junior, employed as an electronics technician with Kuhlmann/Wilhelmshaven, to join Kuhlmann America Inc. for training as my successor. Soon his family, wife and two daughters, arrived. Green Cards were acquired and they bought a house nearby. Horst settled in well. I now had built-up the company to have three employees again, to which we shortly added a fourth, a thirtyish woman for service work and machine demonstrations. A fifth failed and was let go. Turnover increased to just over a million in 1989.

Then Horst was diagnosed with pancreatic cancer, which was removed at the nearby hospital in Hoffman Estates. The surgeon expressed his belief, that he had been able to cut out all cancerous tissue. The average life expectancy for this type of cancer is one year. Because of better social security in Germany, the Zickermanns decided to return there. Horst continued employment, now with Kuhlmann/Bad Lauterberg, the machine tool plant. He survived for another five years!

Yet here I stood again empty-handed! Next year our turnover dropped to a bit over half a million. I gritted my teeth telling myself: "You got to be able to do it!" Well, in 1991, the year I quit my job the middle of November, I had achieved turnover of 1.4 million and had sold 9 CNC machines. By that time I also sold 50% of Kuhlmann's grinder production in the USA. My departure came in handy, since my relationship with Heinz Lossie, the managing director at Kuhlmann, had soured more and more.

Heinz Lossie, never satisfied with 'only' nine annual CNC sales, arranged for Kuhlmann's representation by an American small-type CNC machine maker, Dahlgren, in San Francisco. 60 machines were to be sold by Dahlgren in a year! Five or six demonstrator machines were shipped to the US. But it seems, he didn't quite trust the new setup. I was asked to keep functioning as Kuhlmann America's managing director to oversee things and as liaison, although all physical operations of it had ceased. And, hooray, Dahlgren in January next year received a CNC order from Schindler Elevator, a division of the Swiss parent – one that I had quoted in November and its order promised by the client. Then there were no more sales and also no payments. In the fall of 1992 Kuhlmann withdrew representation and had to take all their demo machines back.

By that time we had moved to Prescott, AZ. Kuhlmann wanted to restart their US-sister, and I agreed to remote-control the new setup in Elk Grove, IL. My old secretary was hired back from Dahlgren, a new technician from Bad Lauterberg was transferred, and a former manager from Newing Hall, a British manufacturer of CNC units, was hired as the manager. For a couple of years, sales limped along with three CNC unit sales annually. Kuhlmann wasn't happy, Barb Wood the secretary, didn't get along with the manager, and so he was fired. The new young fellow we hired didn't produce a single sale in a year and was also let go.

And then thunder struck. Kuhlmann in Bad Lauterberg – Wilhelmshaven had already gone bankrupt – had to file also for chapter 11. Josat and Koch, two individuals, bought Kuhlmann and trimmed it down, also asked me to continue as managing director. That worked for about a year to 1994. I recall this to have been an excellent year for KAI with a net profit before taxes of a bit over $100,000. It was all transferred to the German parent! At that time, Kuhlmann had come up with a big new machine, one to be shown at the Chicago Machine Tool Show, then to go to our showroom. I had successfully contacted oodles and doodles of presidents and vice presidents of machine tool distributors in the US to cover the entire country to represent Kuhlmann for this new piece of equipment. Then the demo unit's return to Germany was requested. When, next year the dollar depreciated rapidly, we had to increase our pricing in the US by 40%, and no assistance was given by the parent, I saw the end coming. Telling the owner, Josat, that he would destroy the company – I quit – again. At the end they sent some jerk from Germany to take over the affairs of KAI, only to get it deeper into morass. Then, Kuhlmann/Germany declared a second bankruptcy, which also meant the end of KAI.

There were several unfinished sales the bankruptcy court would not release without payment including one CNC machine. That's when I offered to pay for these open sales – naturally at my profit. And thus I entered into importing from Kuhlmann to the US. The 'remains' of Kuhlmann were purchased by a German competitor, Lang, near Wetzlar. For a couple of years I consulted for Lang when they explored establishing a new sister company in the USA. During this time I also imported from Lang and in 1997 made the biggest sale of $280,000 to the paper manufacturer Crane in New Hampshire. The equipment served to make the stamping dies for the watermark in the US and other currencies. Together with a 'little' mistake Lang made in billing me, it was enough – even a bit more – to pay for my Lexus RX300 SUV.

Eventually, I helped to establish the US sister, Lang Kuhlmann Inc., and became its temporary vice president. Barely a year later did I part from it, the German parent having fallen into the hands of a yucky new owner. I was out of a job. Nothing deadly about that. We could live. A year later, it turned out, that Lang Kuhlmann Inc. never paid Kuhlmann/Germany for what little they had sold in the US. They needed all they could get their hands on to pay salaries for two and rent, etc. So, Kuhlmann/Germany cut them off. And here came I again.

Since then, until today, I have been importing spare parts, accessories, used and a few new CNC machines from Kuhlmann, also from a Kuhlmann offshoot, Rhotec Computer GmbH. 2000 to 2003 were not much to brag about, the economy had slackened. Annual sales ranged in the neighborhood of $30,000. But the year 2004 produced sales of $112,000, and with a $200,000 CNC unit on order for April 2005, things are looking up. An about 25% gross profit pays for a vacation here and there.

20. Prescott calling

Before 'retiring' late 1991 we had thought of retiring somewhere on the northwest coast. We had purchased a VW van customized in Fort Bragg, CA, to a standup camper. Ute and I flew there to pick it up and drive it home along the coast of California and Oregon, then inland along the Columbia River Valley. Ute found that the humidity along the coast caused her sinus problems, thus we abandoned the idea of moving there. It also turned out, that the infrastructure, hospitals, airports, etc. was still developing.

In the late eighties I had come across a small blurb in Money Magazine about Prescott written by a Pete Dickinson. I had saved it, since the place sounded interesting. Then, when we made our four week camper trip (with two cats) in February of 1992 to explore other places, we stopped in Prescott and fell in love with it. The town, then a burg of about 25,000, had a 'heart', a center as well as ambiance and friendliness of people. We were able to hike up Granite Mountain and Thumb Butte in February! Sure, there was some snow up top, but, gosh, after 22 years in Chicago, cooped up for 4-5 months in winter, we found Prescott a haven. We resolved to come back in June to see what it was like in summer. The first trip took us to Tucson visiting Dirk and Kirsten, and on to Houston, visiting friends. Then we drove on to Jackson, MS, to visit Karen, and home again through a driving snow storm, blowing across the freeway, from southern Illinois all the way home. Ute wanted to find a motel, I stubbornly wanted to get home. Cars, motor homes and trucks were in the ditches left and right, people waving for help, but stopping would have been foolhardy in the driving snow. So I slowly but steadily plugged along.

While in Prescott in February we had come across a beautiful lot in Forest Trails. With the real estate agent not following up and us drifting away from building ourselves, this did not materialize. I put together a detailed listing of desirable features in an existing house, faxed it to another realtor, and when we came again (with two cats) in June, we roamed the Prescott environs house hunting and, after about 20 looks, stepping into 625 Angelita Dr., Ute and I looked at each other in the foyer and knew we had found what we were looking for. On our first visit we had thought to find a house for about $150,000, similar to what we expected to receive for our Schaumburg house, but found that a bit more would be required. We got 625 Angelita Drive for $209,000. The end of August 1992 we moved into a bare house, since our furniture was late. Our two Himalayan cats, Chief and Teetee, loved the empty space while it lasted. The upper floor has 2,400 square feet. Several years ago Dirk put something like a small apartment in the front of the souterrain basement, so that we have now 3,000 sq.ft. Today, as I write this, I think it to be worth more than half a million. We had to shift some investments, sold the third rental in Long Beach, to pay off the mortgages on the other two, and made it possible. No debts!

Right after we moved in at the end of August of 1992 I suggested to Ute to ask her parents to come over. They visited us for three weeks in October and enjoyed the visit and our new house immensely. I just wish my parents would have also been able to see where we finally ended up. Alas...

Mind you, the first years we had to watch our expenditures. We had figured, while still in Schaumburg, that we would have to take on some part-time jobs in Prescott to make ends meet, it was never necessary. And Ute enjoyed her retirement particularly. Nursing would have paid poorly in Prescott.

Not long after our arrival Ute joined the Prescott Art Docents and thus became acquainted with a lot of people. But while these mostly women knew me as Ute's husband (the worse half), I could rarely remember their names (and still do not). We also joined the Newcomers Club and there met Paul and Davida Comba, he a mathematician, she a psychiatrist. Also the Jemisons, both Quakers, both in second marriage, he black, she white. We became friends with both couples, more so with the Combas, since the Jemisons eventually moved away to Sierra Vista and traveled half a year with their motor home. Ute became fast friends with Davida. Paul built an substantial observatory to discover asteroids in the Belt. Several years later, he registered and named two asteroids of the 1000 he had discovered after us. They are Utewindolf, number 20155, discovered by Paul on Oct. 13, 1996 with a revolution of 3.61 years, an absolute magnitude of

16.1, and an estimated diameter of 3 km. The asteroid Herbwindolf, number 20156, also discovered on Oct. 13, 1996, has a revolution of 3.43 years, an absolute magnitude of 15.4 and an estimated diameter of 4 km. When I thanked him upon his announcement at a party I commented that this would likely be the only way I would make it to the heavens!

One friendship led to another and soon there were many. Among them were the Dickinsons, the Money blurb of Pete's having brought us to Prescott. Here and there I flew to Chicago to tend to the affairs of Kuhlmann America, Lang and Lang-Kuhlmann until this petered out. One Chicago visit brought me to Paul Sipiera's wedding.

And while I'm at it, I might as well mention various other travels we undertook. One of the first was with the Sierra Club to Baja California for whale watching. We did one kayak trip across a bay and I knew that kayaking was not for me. I had loved canoeing, but sitting low down in a kayak with legs stretched out forward, was doing nothing for my comfort with the 90° sitting posture it required. But we had the most wonderful halibut ceviche, prepared by our Mexican guides, out on the huge sandbar separating the lagoon from the ocean. Kayaking across the lagoon, a 'knowledgeable' Easterner, a female judge, hearing that we were going to enter the mangrove woods on the opposite side, asked: "Is this where mangos come from?" Walking across the broad sand bar, covered by dunes, we reached the Pacific and found the very smelling carcass of a whale on the beach. Then, hopping across the Sea of Cortez, we took the train ride up Copper Canyon and stayed in a couple of lodges.

In a six week trip with our VW camper we went up the west coast. In Trinidad, a hamlet on the northern California coast, we stopped about lunchtime. While Ute was in a coin wash, I puttered around at the open camper door. A somewhat run-down fellow, sitting by the door of the adjacent post office, held a sign 'Looking for work'. I asked him whether he wanted a peanut butter & jelly sandwich and a coke, to which he responded with "yes". When I handed it to him he said: "God bless you". I think it has been the only time I've been so blessed. But it was nice. Farther north it went through various national parks in British Columbia and Alberta, then through Glacier Park to

Bend, OR, where Karen and Paul were now living, but still without offspring.

Then Ute and I took a self-guided hiking trip in Burgundy and the Alsace. What we most enjoyed were the most stinky, but also most tasty cheeses we could find.

On business travels in the 80s to Kuhlmann in Bad Lauterberg, I was usually the guest of the sales manager, Bruno Schönborn, who enjoyed taking me out for dinner in the evening. To consume 5-6 beers followed by the same number of shots, resulted in me experiencing leakage for a couple of months following each visit. When I established the connection after two years, I refused to partake in Bruno's post-dinner ventures and my troubles disappeared – for several years. Then they popped up again quite severely leading to a virtual stoppage, and since we were scheduled to travel to Zimbabwe where I did not want to end up in a hospital in Harare, I decided to have a T.U.R.P. done, colloquially called a roto-rooter job. This solved the problem somewhat.

The Zimbabwe Safari was a great experience. Among the many, was our three day canoe trip down the Zambesi River, where we must have passed about 2,000 hippos, also crocs, and lots of other wildlife. Afternoons we drifted, having a beer or glass of wine from the cooler, allowing time for the land crew to set up the next camp downstream, tents, shower, flush toilet, dining table – the works. At other camps we stayed, we were able to watch wildlife from hides or took walks through the bush. From the way our guide carried his heavy rifle we could always tell how touchy the situation might be. At one time we faced a herd of cape buffalo, the closest standing about 15 meters distant. It was a first class experience.

At Victoria Falls we took a helicopter ride, too short, to see this wonder from the air. Three times we walked to the park and the Falls to marvel. Our fellow travelers were Steve and Debby Campbell from Glendale, AZ, we only met in Zimbabwe, as well as Christa & Steve from Chicago. The Campbells had previously traveled with them. The two couples decided to take a half-day rafting trip on the lower Zambesi, that is in the gorge below the falls. I had seen two videos of this rafting adventure, had checked with a rafting outfit in the US, and had decided that this was beyond the risk I was prepared to take. And so it was for our fellow-travelers. Their raft capsized and hanging onto the upturned raft, they had to pass the next rapids. The women told us later, that they thought their last minutes had come. And I sure wouldn't have wanted to end up in a Zimbabwean hospital!

At some point Karen and I took a one week trip with the camper, which carried us through upper California and down Big Sur, a drive along the latter I've enjoyed many times. We again stopped in Trinidad, where Karen and I found a nice pair of earrings for Ute. Years later, Ute had lost one of them, she and I stopped by there once more, and the store had a same pair for sale. The saleswoman was prepared to sell us only one, when she heard we had come all the way from Arizona, but I figured two is better than one – yes, having a spare! And while I'm hopping back and forth between two trips here – when I had lunch with Karen at the Wharf in San Francisco, I ordered Chiopino. With a bib around my neck and tomato sauce around my mouth, Karen had to take a picture of her messy father, as she had never seen him before. Oh, and in a third trip with Kirsten up the coast going to Bend, we stopped at Agate Beach, where Ute and I in a previous trip and at low tide had found quite a few agates. This time, with Kirsten, the tide was in and our finds were poor. But Kirsten was so taken by the colorful pebbles, that she first filled two plastic bags, and when these were full, took off her poncho in the misty, cool morning, and filled the poncho with lots and lots of pebbles.

Some time, in the late 1990s I joined Jack Solomon and his son David, as well as Jack's nephew, Milton Schild, to go up 12,600 ft high Humphrey's Peak, the highest one of the San Franciscos. But one starts this ascend at 9,000 ft. Jack, the oldest of our little group, dropped out at about the halfway point. Eventually, when we got to steep switch-backs, I told the two younger ones, in their 40s, to go ahead, not to slow down because of me. Which they did. When I got to the saddle, above the tree line, I could see them still ahead of me, also a small thunderstorm moving in. The two made it in time. I was still about 300 ft below the summit, when lightning caused me to retreat. Shucks! My drive home with Jack and Milton, David lived in Flagstaff at the time, was one of the toughest drives I ever did – from tiredness. My two passengers slept, but I had to fight staying awake.

Two years later, it may have been in 2000, Ute was in Bend, I thought to try it again – solo. No one to hold me back, no one I would have to tell: go ahead. I told Ute and Kirsten what I was up to, had brewed myself a thermos of black coffee, and left Prescott about 5 AM. So, by 7 AM I began my ascent. I might have met at most 10 people on the way up and on the summit, where the wind blew so fiercely that my hiking stick slanted sideways every time I lifted it off the ground. But I got up there.

I took this trip on a Saturday which meant that .... on the way down, I must have passed about 200 people attempting their late ascent, among them was Steve Campbell of Zimbabwe fame. And I drank the whole darn thermos full of coffee and drove home without being tired.

Subsequently, Ute and I took our one and only cruise through the Society Islands, starting in Tahiti. Boating through the lagoon on Morea we passed the Club Med facilities and found that the environment had suffered during the intervening years. Yet on Bora Bora we swam with about 20-25 rays and watched sharks being fed while we floated a little distance away in the water.

A guided tour next year took us for a few days to Florence, then on hikes through Tuscany, Cinque Terre and Umbria, ending in Rome. On our way home we stopped in Bad Marienberg, where Ute's parents stayed in a retirement home. Two weeks later Ute had to return there for her father's burial!

It must have been in 2000, that we, together with Gene & Lynn Chesson, neighbors and friends, were set to travel to Morocco with Overseas Adventure Travels. Davida Comba, Ute's, our friend, was terminally ill from cancer she had fought for more than two decades. When it looked that she might die soon, Ute cancelled to remain in Prescott. I took off with the Chessons and, among other things, experienced the northern reaches of the Sahara, climbing one of the highest sand dunes around. Our guide, a Moroccan, with a BA in English literature, and pretty much Westernized, but whenever called for, wore Moroccan garb, was pretty open. He told us once in a respective setting, that he had to sacrifice a chicken to demonstrate to his in-laws, that he had married a virgin. Upon parting at the Casablanca airport, I was the only one, as far as I could see, he said farewell to the Arab way, cheek to cheek. I do not know why he did it – but once more – I felt honored! Then, after our return, Davida hung on for another year, but when she was failing again, just before our planned Turkey trip, Ute decided to go.

Thus, in 2001, three weeks after 9/11, we flew out of New York with Turkish Airlines to Istanbul. Another flight took us to central Anatolia, the city of Kaycera, from there by bus to Antalya on the southern coast. We skippered along the coast in a 'gulet', a small motorized sailboat. Another bus ride brought us to the ruins of Ephesus and a flight to Istanbul. We walked the Grand Bazar and the Spice Market, having become comfortable with the sometimes pushy merchants and just kidded with them. In a walk from the Bazar to the Spice Market we were the only Westerners.

In the summer of 2002 a friend gathered a group of people to hike Paria Canyon, the Paria River being a tributary to the Colorado River. It runs north-south, entering the Colorado near Lee's Ferry in Arizona. There were five intrepid hikers, and five, well, less intrepid ones. Ute and I, Grant Brown, and the Neals resolved to hike only part of the canyon, explore a bit farther south from a base camp, and then return to our departure point. Ute carried 35 pounds plus her camera gear, I carried 42, lots of it being water. And we carried no tents, slept on a tarp, and when it drizzled one night, just pulled out the tarp from under us and put it on top. Well, why not. We had traveled the Grand Canyon twice without tents – almost. The Paria flowed low, at most a few inches deep, which is why we had selected to enter the canyon at the time. Yet for most of the time we walked in water. There was also quicksand, and once I had to be pulled out, having sunk with one leg in up to my thigh. It's clinging stuff!

Then we wanted to float down the Colorado once more to see what it would be like 20 years later. Kirsten, had just finished her Master's, and got the trip as her prize. Steve and Debby Campbell also came along. They also bought our VW camper when I had enough of it.

This was a much smaller group than on our previous trip, maybe only 8-10. I found that the 20 years that had elapsed had made the trip harder. I developed swelling of the hands and lower legs and could fall asleep sitting on rocks. After we got back I saw a cardiologist for a stress test. It turned out okay, but he told me that, from my description, I might have come close to congestive heart failure. Its cause may have been the additional salt that was fed us by the crew in the Canyon. At that time I had already been going for two years to workouts, had added an inch to my shoulder width, and had kept my blood pressure below 140/90. A few months later my blood pressure suddenly jumped to 180/110 and I was put on the hypertension meds Altace and a diuretic.

And this May of 2004 we took another selfguided tour in Provence with our friend and neighbor, Grant Brown, eighty years of age. After the one-week hike we flew to Munich, visited with the Liesners, then took our rented car up the Romantic Road to Dinkelsbühl and Rothenburg. In an overnight stay in Jagsthausen at the castle of the Berlichingens, we enjoyed a wonderful meal in the castle restaurant. I also learned then that the elder Berlichingen, one year younger than I, had already died ten years ago. When I stayed in Jagsthausen at the end of the War, our gang of 7-8-9 year olds had roamed with him the castle grounds among other places.

I now must be careful what I say here, not because of the Nazi issue, but the 'jesting relationship'. In Nazi-times most Germans pursued genealogy to determine whether some Jewish ancestry might lurk in the past. As stated earlier, my maternal ancestors came from Jagsthausen. It was found, that in the mid-seventeen hundreds a woman, unmarried, employed at the court of the Götz von Berlichingen, had two children! It did not take long for this find to become public knowledge in the small village of Jagsthausen, and when my mother, her brother or sister came visiting, they were often greeted with: Oh, here come the Götz's children! If this is true, then, maybe, this is where my irreverence comes from. Remember my earlier report on one of the Götz sticking his butt out a window and inviting the besieging army's colonel to lick ....

When we arrived in Bad Mariental we learned that Ute's mother had died the day before. Ute stayed to assist in the funeral arrangements. I drove north with Grant, but then dashed back a day for the internment. Ute flew home, and Grant and I visited two others, Bruno Schönborn's widow, and Hans Möhlmann in Wilhelmshaven. Up there, I also wanted to taste Dover sole once more, as I had in the past whenever I stayed there for business. It turned out, that only baby soles were available any longer due to overfishing. Terrible – to eat babies!

In 2003 and 04 we spent a couple of weeks each at the very pretty place of our friend, Anne Schwerdt, right beside the Frying Pan River in Colorado near Aspen.

In 2005 we are booked, I for my fifth, Ute for her third trip to Africa. For almost the entire month of June we will be traveling with a small group by land through Namibia, then by ourselves fly between three camps in Botswana, to finally end up in Cape Town. Recently mentioning our plans to some friends, former Germans, Irene Schuring brought out a book written by a German about his exploits in Namibia in the late 30s, early 1940s. Its title: "Wenn es Krieg gibt, gehen wir in die Wüste", translating to: "When War breaks out, we'll head for the Desert." I enjoyed it very much and recommended it to Ute. Two places named in the book we shall see. I found out on the Internet, that an English translation exists with the title "The Sheltering Desert". Now I don't need to translate it. An English copy has just arrived.

21. Second Opening Up.

About a year after our arrival in Prescott I was approached by a neighbor, Bob Stragnell, whether I would be interested and considered myself in a position to translate a book written in the late 1840s by a German by the name of Ehrenberg. It's name was: "The Texas War of Independence in 1848". This book had been published in several editions in Germany in the middle of that century, and was thought to have contributed substantially to the influx of German immigrants to the Austin, Texas, area. 1998 was the 150s anniversary of this epochal event and Bob hoped to get it published by one of the Texas university presses.

I set to work, eventually delivered it to him, and he contacted 'Texas'. As it turned out, however, the major university there had already contracted with two university professors, fluent in German, and my labors were for naught. My translation is still in my computer, should anyone wish to publish it for the 200rds anniversary in 2048. The little town of Ehrenberg by the Colorado River in Arizona is named after the author by the grace of the Goldwaters. Nevertheless, the translating process, as well as the historic events recounted in the book, were of great interest to me.

Then an article on Karl May, hero of my youth, appeared in our local newspaper, The Courier, in which the author, a   third generation Prescottonian, was looking for a translator of Karl May's 'The Oil Prince'. This is May's only novel playing entirely in the state, then territory of Arizona. Prescott was mentioned several times in it. I responded, and since Bill Bork, this year 98 years old, knew Bob Stragnell very well, and I offered to do the job for free, I got it. As of today, it is my only translation that has been published in 2002 by Washington State University Press.

That same year I translated May's 'The Treasure of Silver Lake', but have so far not found a publisher.

Around that time an American submariner delivered to me the diary of a German U-boat-man, whose boat was sunk in the Caribbean, The fellow POWd in various camps in the US, finally landing in Tempe, AZ. That's were about 25 U-boaters made the largest escape of any POW camp in the USA. They must have done it from sheer boredom, since there was really no incentive to get back into the schlimazel. They dug through the hard-as-concrete caliche and underneath an irrigation canal. A couple of them had built an inflatable boat, thinking to raft down the Salt River. Ha, when they got there it, as usual, carried no water. Needless to say, they were all caught again. One of our neighbors, Bill Pedersen, as an 18 year old US soldier, was a guard at the camp. Just the other day I translated a Christmas card, written by the widow of one of the U-boat-men he had become friends with. Many back and forth visits of numerous PoWs took place in the post-war years. This translation has been incorporated in the collection of the Historical Society of Phoenix and Tucson. In a side note: The hand picking record of cotton in Arizona is still held by German U-boaters and mariners.

A bit later I was contacted by a local woman whose German ancestor, Anna Mugler, having lived in Lawrence, Kansas, had written a series of poems in the German Sütterlin script in the mid-1860s. So I set to work, first transcribing it in German to the Latin script, then into English, and subsequently putting it into some verse form.

The translations of various correspondences and critiques of and about the surrealist artist Fred Sommer with Dieter Wyss in Germany followed.

When Davida Comba had died, her husband Paul, my friend, asked me to give the eulogy. I had never done something like this. The two times I had to speak publicly in a professional context, I thought to have done quite badly. My concern was always to either not remember all that was to be said or to get out of sequence. So I begged out of giving the eulogy! And I felt badly afterwards!

Two, two and one half years ago, I joined the then-called Yavapai Learning Institute, nowadays the Osher Lifelong Learning Institute for some courses. A seat neighbor, Walt Bull, who turned out to also be a facilitator (giving courses), mentioned to me that it was difficult getting new subjects to present. I said, that shouldn't be so hard. I wrote up a brief summary of five or six subjects I could think of and handed them to him next time. Within a week Leslie Parsons from the Institute called me, asking: "Which of these subjects would you like to facilitate next semester?" And thus I was shanghaied into another task. A strong parallel reason for me to join was – that I would have to speak publicly. I had to overcome my deficiency. And so, I did. Yet, I still prefer to read my course material, although I always hand it out also to all my participants. But I've learned to speak freely in the interactions and breaks of my readings.

Since then I have given courses with the titles: From the Spice Trade to Globalization, Cataclysms & Extinctions, Water: The Elixir of Life, Human Evolution and Migration, The American National Mind vis-à-vis the Rest of the World, which I did twice, To the Cambrian Explosion & Beyond, and The Likely Futility of S.E.T.I. Programs. And then I experienced what, for sake of a better term I must call burnout, a condition I'm still in when it comes to preparing future courses.

All my courses I assembled from scratch, starting with a basic knowledge and interest in the subject material, then gathering additional information from scientific and popular publications and the internet. Whenever possible I tried to introduce to my course participants, all elderly folks, new ideas, new findings, something not readily known, like the Snowball Earth theory, the importance of the Moon on the Earth's stability, etc. Assembling this material and integrating it has added very much to my personal knowledge. But in collecting the latest research, I have come across so many negative findings, that it became somewhat depressing. I tried to convey to my 'students' that the universe is a violent place, not so hunky-dory as we see it. Then I emphasized our need to learn to think, as far as that is possible, in Deep Time, backward and forward, in thousands, millions, even tens and hundreds of million years. And the more I gathered data, the more I became aware of how little I truly know, can know, of the utter complexity our world, our universe is comprised of. Who am I to give courses on these complexities? I know, that I know quite a lot, more than most of my course participants, and yet...

I had promised the Osher Institute's News Editor, Eve Wynant, to give a course of oceanography in Spring 1 of 2005, but had to beg out. For weeks now I have been unable to 'get to it', although I have the course half finished. But I did promise it to Eve, therefore, I must 'get to it' to get it done for Spring 2, for Eve is 91 years old and has told me that, if I wait too long, she may no longer be around. That's some pressure!

I have other courses in various stages of preparation: Salt: The Essence of Life, Soil: It's just Dirt! Or is it?, and From Baby Boom to Baby Bust. And there are so many other subjects I could address like Language, Ethics, and Heritage of the Western World. I think those final ones will tax me too much, so, if I could finish with Salt, Soil and Babies, I should have done my share.

I got to know good people in the course of giving these courses and I got additional ones to join the Institute. One of the cute experiences in this context has been that, when years ago we went to the symphony concerts at Prescott's Yavapai Performance Hall, and stepped out for intermission, I all too often didn't know all these people Ute knew from the Art Docents. The tables were turned, when Ute didn't know my course participants and fellow-facilitators.

In the context of these, my Remembrances, let me slip in, that the Osher quarterly newsletter a couple of years ago request a mini-autobiography of mine for publication. Recently, I was interviewed by a local freelance journalist and landscape photographer, Pete Peters, for a biography, that was published in Lovin' Life News. And Gene and George Toor at Osher want me to give a talk on my 'life's experiences' in an upcoming course of theirs were various people talk about themselves. I don't know what this is all about. Sure, I think I've had a full and interesting life, but I can think of many others, who experienced more or greater things.

In the last issue the Osher Quarterly published my little travelogue on our hike in Provence, which also appeared in Paul Sipiera's Planetary Studies Foundation Newsletter. They published already a short essay of mine on Snowball Earth. Other articles are in wait. And I will certainly write one on our Namibia/Botswana safari.

Thus, in the past year I have become very relaxed with people, even strangers. Ute has called me – me – a social butterfly. Me, the introvert for most of my life, shy in youth, later all too often a bit 'off' in social matters. I have become very comfortable, can banter even with strangers, that I have recently said: One of these days, someone will punch me in the nose for kidding him. America has been good to/for me. What it has taught, is still teaching, is the acceptance of others and the self! I have come to enjoy people.

By one connection leading to another I have become part of a foursome of male friends. Al Herron, the only native-born American of our group, a former hospital administrator, Nigel Reynolds and Manfred Wenner, both naturalized citizens of the US, the former, with a name like Nigel, from Britain, the latter, with a Ph.D. in Political Sciences, came from Switzerland. And he's a radical par excellence! Every two to three weeks we get together in rotation at our homes to vigorously and boisterously discuss all kinds of subjects. Nigel and Manfred, or Kurt, as he's also called, are more interested in 'hard' subjects, whereas Al and I are also intrigued by 'soft 'or 'fuzzy' issues, not so easy to pin down.

Earlier this year, actually, today is the first day of 2005, so it was last year, we gave a potluck party for about 40 friends at our house, and we could have added a few more. The Harringtons, our first friends from Canada, now living in Indiana, flew in from there. Kirsten and Felipe came up from Tucson, and the Campbells from Glendale.

With Ute having traveled quite a bit during the past two years to see her mother in Germany as well as her ailing, then dying sister, Christa, in Long Beach, I stayed home house and cat-sitting. Frequently did I then invite friends for dinners, which I cooked, one recipe downloaded from the internet. But Ute is the cook par excellence. I can never touch her – when it comes to cooking!

One other thought. I have a dichotomous relationship with rituals, any ritual! I understand their value for social cohesion, can feel shivers going down my spine when a national anthem is being sung, any anthem, but simultaneously resent their captivating powers. When doing yoga I do not care to assume the prayer pose, etc., etc. Ritual impinges on my personal freedom! In my collection of aphorisms and adages I have included the:

Tao Te Ching
When the Tao is lost there is Goodness,
When Goodness is lost there is Kindness,
When Kindness is lost there is Justice,
When Justice is lost there is Ritual.
Ritual is the Husk of Faith and Hope
and the Beginning of Chaos.

Let me attach some health issues here. Until age 50 I used to joke that my eyesight was the only sense still functioning. Then I needed glasses. In my forties, in Schaumburg, I encountered episodes of what must have been rheumatoid arthritis particularly in my wrists. These became at times so bad, that I was unable to lift myself out from the edge of the communal swimming pool. It popped up in other parts of the body and, interestingly, disappeared totally after a few years. But the curse of ageing of all creatures expressed itself eventually in osteoarthritis, not that it became debilitating.

I have been diagnosed with the beginnings of glaucoma and dry macular degeneration and do whatever can be done to keep it in check. Cataracts are something relatively easy to take care of. And, what seems to be a genetic characteristic, high blood pressure, has also popped up a few years ago. If no accident should happen this is, despite medication, I think, what eventually will get the better of me.

22. Companions.

I cannot complete this story without mentioning our oh-so-short-lived cat companions of many years. Here I need to say how ignorant we were decades ago taking care of pets. And not only in these matters did we lack knowledge and experience.

My preference has always been cats. Dogs are pride animals, they want attention and live with submission. I would have been the lead dog. That I did not care for. Give me a cat who tells me: Take it or leave it! A being more in its own right, solitary by nature, yet also needing company. Their affection I perceived to be displayed in their own interest. As an Irish saying goes: A cat purrs for its own good self.

Our first cat in Canada, I don't even recall her name, was somewhat neurotic. Maybe she expressed a bit the environment she lived in. We couldn't or wouldn't afford to have her spayed, funds were dear. But of the set of kittens we had once I had to drown two. And not that I liked it. When we left Canada, we had to turn her in to a shelter.

Years later, in Schaumburg, the kids came home with a foundling, a little gray tabby they had picked up on a parking lot and promised to take care of 'forever'. Well, as those things turn out, when they left, one after the other, Schmuppi, as they had called the fellow, became our cat. He was an outdoor feline, but usually came in for the night. When I then sat in my easy-chair, my feet on the footstool, he used to stretch out on my outstretched legs and fall asleep, eventually turning upside down. We had a very accepting relationship. Often did I later say, that there had been only to beings in my live who transmitted to me the feeling of total acceptance – my mother and Schmuppi! I loved this character – and when he caught feline leukemia and wasted away, became incontinent, and was sure to die – I killed him myself by wrapping him into a sheet, then pressing him to my heart to suffocate him. His struggles were feeble and brief. I buried him on our lot. I had been afraid that, if we would go to a vet to have him euthanized, I would not be able to take him home. That day, I destroyed all utensils related to him.

Yet, I think within a year I happened to see a creme-colored sealpoint Himalayan kitten in a pet shop – and fell in love again for $400. And thus we got Chief, derived from mischief. We let him get out in the yard, which we should not have. He picked something up, needed to be shorn, and as he grew older, became, what we called a high-maintenance cat. The get him company, we 'rescued' another male bluepoint Himalayan from another pet shop. His name went from Prince through Etee to Teetee. He had been too cute for his own good in the pet shop and must have 'suffered' too much attention from visitors. He was always shy and deliberate. Of Teetee's demise I have written a letter, in which I discharged my guilt and grief of his death. You will find it as an attachment. Chief became ill so that he had to be given prednozone on a regular basis. When he eventually refused to take it, then refused food, even water, and we had to leave on a trip, we took him to our vet. Amen. They are both buried on our lot.

Thereafter, we decided to get two tabby successors from the humane society, this time two females, Spunky and Hidie, both named after their chief characteristic. Spunky sleeps with us, mostly Ute, actually, and Hidie, when she's not hiding, talks with us, due to her part Siamese ancestry. We have always had friends come in to feed them, even sit with them when we went on trips. But it was all to apparent, that they suffered, moped, already when we packed. So, when we go for four weeks to southern Africa in June of 2005, we arranged with Kirsten to come up to our house as 'cat company'. They are now eight years old and we will likely not get another set when their lives have come to an end, for we too may not outlive a new set. And who would take care of them when we are gone?! We would also like to see it possible for Karen, Natalie and Emma with their allergies to be able to visit us at our home.

The older I became, the more I have seen these beings as semiconscious creatures owed respect – and not just that.

23. Where now, and still where to?

Each of us five did set out on our own search to understand ourselves and the world we live in. Yet while the 'other' four all appear to have found the one or other 'teacher', I have always thought of this being a task for my very self. I have picked and chosen from insights I have come across, readings, movies, friends, sufferings, joys, and whatever. My task has been and still is to assemble, to integrate what is to be learned and to make it my very own. Thus, one day, I can say: I did it myself!

Following is, however, my favorite poem – not that I have many – of Rudyard Kipling, the British 'Poet of Empire', as he was called. Ute never cared for it much, but I've understood it always as a lead to follow, an exhortation, something to strive for, to approach, but maybe to succeed at only in part. Could it be, that it requires a saint to achieve it in its entirety? I am by far no saint! And yet...

If
by Rudyard Kipling

If you can keep your head when all about you are losing
theirs and blaming it on you;
If you can trust yourself when all men doubt you, but make allowance
for their doubting too:
If you can wait and not be tired of waiting, or, being lied about, don't
deal in lies, or being hated don't give way to hating, and yet don't look
to good, nor talk too wise;
If you can dream - and not make dreams your master;
If you can think - and not make thoughts your aim;
If you can meet with Triumph and Disaster and treat those tw
impostors just the same;
If you can bear to have the truth you've spoken twisted by knaves
to make a trap for fools, or watch the things you gave your life to,
broken, and stoop and buiid'm up with worn out tools;
If you can make one heap of all your winnings and risk it on one turn
of pitch-and-toss, and lose, and start again at your beginnings, and
never breathe a word about your loss:

If you can force your heart and nerve and sinew to serve your turn
long after they are gone, and so hold on when there is nothing in you
except the Will which says to them "Hold on!"
If you can talk with crowds and keep your virtue, or walk with Kings -
nor lose the common touch;
If neither foes nor loving friends can hurt you,
If all men count with you, but none too much;
If you can fill the unforgiving minute with sixty seconds' worth
of distance run, Yours is the Earth and everything that's in it.
And - which is more - you'll be a man, my son!

And while this poem answers some questions, a statement of
one of my "favorite Jewish scientists", Richard Feynman – I have a
number of admired Jewish scientists, such as Stephen Gould , Jared
Diamond, and others – succinctly expresses another of my beliefs.

"You see, one thing is, I can live with doubt and uncertainty and not
knowing.
I think it's much more interesting to live not knowing than to have
answers which might be wrong. I have approximate answers and
possible beliefs and different degrees of certainty about different things,
but I'm not absolutely sure of anything and there are many things I
don't know anything about, such as whether it means anything to ask
why we're here ...
I don't have to know an answer. I don't feel frightened by not knowing
things, by being lost in a mysterious universe without any purpose,
which is the way it really is as far as I can tell. It doesn't frighten me."

Since my early teens I have been interested in the sciences,
astronomy, cosmology, geology, oceanography, anthropology,
economics, history, sociology, psych, and more. Yet, my lack of
patience would never have made a scientist out of me – as it has been
shown. The pursuit of science matters can be a grubby business, so, in
later years I have called myself a "would-have-liked-to-be-scientist".
And the sciences' offspring, technology, has always been of interest to
me, but only in general terms. I think, my experience in the 'blue-collar
world' injected early enough the wish not to involve myself in technical
aspects, the repair of a car, etc., etc. In later years it became important

for me to have others do these kinds of jobs for me and to be able to pay to have them done.

Nevertheless, I think I can call myself a Scientific Materialist! But I am no radical. I know there is much beyond accepted scientific approaches that is poorly understood or not at all. One aspect of this was expressed by J.B.S. Haldane in: "The universe is not only weirder than we think; it is weirder than we can think." Yet this statement does not cover the fuzzy aspects of the mind, of consciousness, the activity of healers, universal consciousness, water molecules seemingly influences by mind projections, telepathy, etc. I have suspended judgment on these matters, have decided, that to enter into these realms requires leaving scientific materialism behind in order to maybe, just maybe, experience the one or the other phenomenon. I find it not worthwhile! So I have decided to stick with the accessible and to leave belief into these phenomena to others. It's not my cup of tea.

From my anthropological background I wager that all deities beholden on this planet have been created by man, from 'simple' beginnings in the dim past to greater elaborations once agrarian societies, and with their rise, the state came into being. Based on the complexities of the universe as we know them to be, but remember Haldane's above statement, I consider it to be either the ultimate hubris or the ultimate folly for man to imagine any deity and to assign it certain characteristics.

The above is very much connected with the evolution of our consciousness, feeble, animal-like at the beginning, two, three million years ago, but having grown to our today's complexity. Whether the evolution of this feature is accidental, or part of a greater scheme of evolution, is not for us to fathom. If we decide it to be part of something greater, to be part of a 'universal spirit', then we will find out soon enough. But it is not something to worry about. It's no use anyway. And if, with our death, that consciousness is gone, then, so be it! But if this is correct, then it is ever more important to fill this life with everything we've got and, maybe, leave it a bit better than we found it. For myself, I think I can say to have had a good, a fortunate life. I think, that when the time comes to leave it, I can do so without upheaval, though not without some regrets and some sorrow. So be it!

One of my personal practical mottos has been: "If I'm not ahead, I will be behind." Trying to think ahead, to anticipate, and without ever having been a boy scout or Coast Guard member assumed their motto: Semper paratus – always prepared. And it has served me well! Mind you, some of these adages crystalized only over the years, particularly my later years. But some I must have already followed long ago yet without having put them into words.

I've had some sleepless nights these past weeks. The night of the 30s of December 2004, and not only that night, I was almost entirely awake, remembering and composing in my mind the sentences I was to put down. I felt driven! Thus I wrote these Remembrances in the course of only about three weeks. Ah, yes, I'm fast, also impatient, two characteristics which many times were my curse and my strength. The above adage I have quoted many a times has been: If I'm not ahead, I will be behind. Yet I never left quality out of my eyes, also knew when to let go, to be flexible. One of my most important pursuits has been to always look for Solutions. Solutions usually require compromise.

From time to time there will be now some additions as things transpire.

This March of 2005 I flew to Chicago for Paul Sipiera's and his Planetary Studies Foundation annual benefit dinner with about 200 people attending, some of the big shots, one of them a member of the Chicago Pritzkers. Paul and Diane, his wife, put me up at their house, also Birgit Sattler from Austria, and Trevor Ireland from Australia (he's actually a Kiwi), an old friend of Paul's from his study years at the University of Otago in Dunedin, New Zealand, I had also met several times in the past. He was on his way to Houston for a meeting with NASA people.

The keynote speaker at the dinner was Scott Carpenter, a Mercury astronaut, I had the honor to ferry around a few times. His two

313

heroes were Jack Kennedy and Wernher von Braun he mentioned in private and public.

I also invited Paul for dinner at Jim Lovell's (of Apollo 13 fame) fancy French restaurant north of Chicago, where Paul was shepherding ten $500/piece benefit diners downstairs. Paul's and mine was cheap at hundred and eighty.

When I shook hands with Jim Lovell I was extremely tempted to tell him, that I thought Tom Hanks had done a better job bringing Apollo 13 back, but my 'inborn reverence' and respect prevented me from saying that. Who knows, he may have also kicked me out of his establishment which, incidentally, is run by his son. It is ironic though, as I learned afterward from Scott Carpenter, that the Apollo 13 crew got recognition from the White House only after the release of the movie! Before, it had always been NASA's policy to keep 'failures' out of the limelight. But, hell, a failure can also be a supreme accomplishment. It is also sad to see how old these guys have become. We sure need some fresh ones!

24. And on it goes.

Where do I start? Almost a year has passed and a few developments can be added to this ongoing story.

I have written several travelogues about our safari in southern Africa during the month of June 2005, which are attached. Still pending is my attempt to get a medical team to Namibia to check local people for eye problems and do surgery. One of the two Canadian women, Marty, we met in Cape Town, told about their volunteer service for MMI, Medical Ministry International, in northern Mozambique, from where they had just returned. MMI is a Christian-based organization sending volunteer doctor teams to developing countries for up to 15 different medical procedures. It can take up to two years to field such a team. They also set up permanent facilities in recipient countries, educating and training locals to perform these services. Mary had given me a pamphlet on MMI.

Upon our return I called their offices in Texas, left my name and address and, within half an hour, had an e-mail response from their international director, at the time fielding a team in Peru. Within a couple of hours through multiple e-mails, it was established that MMI would field a team of 10 doctors to Namibia for two weeks. However, only two days would be required to check and treat the 300 Topnar members of Rudolf Dausab's tribe. And MMI would need an invitation from a tribal council in Namibia to go there.

This was initiated in mid-July. It is now the end of October 2005, and I'm still waiting to see this invitation. Africa's mills grind slowly! My airmail parcel with 17 eye glasses took two months to be delivered. Rudolf is still waiting for a confirmation of cooperation from the Namibian Health Dept. He also needs/needed to get other tribes involved to make fielding a team worthwhile.

MMI's director, Willie Hunter visited me in Prescott. On leaving he told me that I was the first individual trying to get something like this going. If I could pray, I would for this venture to succeed.

There was the question of accommodating, transporting and feeding the med team. Rudolf, in e-mail exchanges, said he could take care of the first two. I offered to gather the funds for feeding, amounting to about $ 4,000. Well, I got pledges from friends, relatives, and myself for $ 5,000 so far.

315

By now I have also three Karl May translations in print: The Oil Prince, The Treasure of Silver Lake, and The Ghost of Llano Estacado. A forth is in the works, to be done in early 2006. Its German title is Winnetou IV – terrible title. I suppose I shall name it "Winnetou's Heirs". I don't expect to become rich from these translations. It's a past time and, actually, will cost me more than is coming in. Anyway, I just got my first quarterly royalty check for The Treasure for $ 30. Hahaha, who knows? I guess four May translation will then be enough. I might get otherwise cross-eyed. But then – one never knows.

In the process – oh, I got also a new big-screen Mac, so that I can have German and English side-by-side – I have established a lively e-mail interchange with my publisher, other Karl May aficionados, Dr. Bill Thomas in Melbourne, Australia, and Marlies Bugmann in Tasmania, a 'Jackie' of all trades. Hurray to e-mail!

I have been elected Exec. VP and to the board of Paul Sipiera's Planetary Studies Foundation (PSF), which will require my occasional attendance at board meetings in Chicago.

A few weeks ago I did with Grant Brown the 11 mile hike up Pine Mountain, without having walked much and not hiked at all in the months before. It was a tough hike, but I can still do it. I just had to see if, what I said earlier, one can 'see forever' from up there. It's close!

Karen, with her presently six and three year old daughters, Natalie and Emma, has separated from her husband, Paul, and is now filing for divorce. Now she's got a disbanded engagement and two marriages behind her.

Kirsten got Ute's Accord after her car got totaled in a rear-ending by a California woman. In place Ute got a brand new allwheel drive Subaru LLBean Outback and I need to have less concern when she's driving during our occasional ice and snow conditions.

For August 2006 I have booked us for an Alaska tour, flying to Fairbanks, taking a train and bus through Denali to Anchorage then, with a 100 passenger boat through Glacier Bay (before the glaciers all melt) and the Inland Passage to Vancouver and home.

I cannot bring myself (at this time) to give any more classes at Osher. But I will take one with Dieter Schuring on Existentialism. For it, I still need to write a short essay for presentation. Somehow my participation got triggered in conversations with Dieter, who is 83, has had colon cancer, now metastases in the liver, and beginning Parkinson's.

It appears my attempt at getting a medical team to Namibia will not materialize. My contact there seems to have given up. Africa again!

My own eyesight isn't getting any better. I now need stronger drops for my glaucoma. My double vision, having troubled me for several years, has now been alleviated by prisms in my glasses. Ah, well!

On December 15, 2005 I picked up a new Lexus RX400h, trading in my old one. This Hybrid ought to last me for the rest of my driving life. But who knows.

The Alaska trip is behind us and my travelogue was published in the PSF Quarterly Newsletter. For January 2007 I have booked us for a trip around the Galapagos Islands on a small 12 passenger boat. Got to do it while I/we can. Then, in July of 2007 Ute is arranging for a family reunion on Kauai. In September/October we will visit Germany for three weeks. I have plans to invite Kirsten and Felipe to join us on a trip to Costa Rica in the spring of 2008; in fall of this year we intend to rent a place somewhere in Idaho or Montana for a couple of weeks where Karen can join us with her girls for a week. And I would love to still go on a hiking tour in the Dordogne! Oh, that French cheese! So it goes on.

Karen has her divorce now behind her, but the emotional stuff will hang on for some time.

Now, in 2006, we sold the Volk property in Long Beach for $490,000, which we had purchased in 1976 for $47,000. The 20+ year

317

renters of Tulane have signed a Lease To Purchase contract for this property, which ought to be consummated on June 30, 2009 for $535,000, when we purchased it in 1983 for $105,000. Hopefully the proceeds will last us to the end of our lives, if we don't spend it on travels.

I'm also now on the board of our local Yavapai Symphony Association for the duration of three years, and have 6 Karl May translations in print, working on another one. There's shortly another trip to Chicago due for another of Paul's benefit dinners with Jack Lousma of Skylab fame the guest speaker.

We have our Galapagos trip behind us, my travelogue waiting to appear in the PSF Quarterly. Now I'm thinking of doing a private Wilderness trip to Costa Rica in 2008 with Ute, Kirsten and Felipe. For this year, Ute will take us yet on a family reunion for a week's stay to a private beech house on Kauai. In fall we intend to visit Ute's brother, Michael with his wife Wilja, my friend Hand Moehlmann, and Ute's sister, Doerthe, with her husband in Berlin. The beginning of May, I'll go on a three day hiking trip around Page, AZ. Enuff of travel plans.

25. Pursuing Sophia

To interconnect knowledge, integrating ethics and, most of all bringing in, what is sometimes called 'heart', the three forming a whole, then applying them to the manifold issues of life, may constitute the beginning of wisdom. The above 'cute' title actually speaks of an impossibility: One cannot pursue sophia. I feel it is rather a quality arising from within, from a deeper being, building little by little, some from painful, some from joyful experiences, some from facts. If I chose this title, which may confuse some people, it is to say that this 'pursuit' must include also a certain playfulness. Sophia need not be all serious.

For over a year now I have been in e-mail exchange with my Tasmanian coconspirator in translating Karl May novels. She has been / is of great help in getting two more into print. Aside from our 'professional' exchanges, we have addressed many personal aspects. In the course, Marlies Bugmann expressed her belief that the universe is all 'spirit'. Okay, chaque un a son goût!, but her belief, and not only this one, is 'firm', total, absolute. As a consequence of these exchanges, I delved a bit more into where I stand. Nothing really new now, just 'firmed' up.

Marlies 'knows', whereas 'I do not'!

I'm talking here of a philosophical stance. It does not imply that she knows everything, whereas I know nothing, no, it's just that I do not claim to ever have total assuredness. There's only one: Death.

When I recently went as moral support to a friend's, Nigel Reynolds, debate with a creationist, then, walking early across the parking lot of the venue, a church (of all places), I met a stranger also entering. I introduced myself, handing him my card. He, in turn, pulled also out a little card, like a business card, and handed it to me. Reading some of it, I noticed it's sentences were exhortations to believe in Jesus and God. I handed it back to him, suggesting to keep it for a worthier fellow. He then asked me: Don't you have any trust? At first, puzzled by the question, I retorted eventually: I only have trust in that there is no certainty! That closed our conversation.

And yet, while I'm at it. I've translated, in addition to May's novels, also a number of his poems. His last one, written about two months before his death in 1912, has touched and keeps touching me profoundly every time I read it. While I'm not a man of his persuasion, a Christian, I can appreciate it for where he came from. I think, I also succeeded well in my translation. It will be published entitled "Reflections" as the final page of my translation of his last novel, Winnetou's Heirs, some time towards the end of 2006. I read this poem at Dieter's funeral.

At the beginning of these, my Remembrances, I tell about my "spiritual" experience on the jetty in Sweden, an experience never to be repeated. I have often wondered why, even regretted having had no repeats. I think I have now an explanation: At the age of my experience I was 17 years old, still in the process of development. I had always been interested by the sciences, 'ratio', disdaining what I perceived as too emotional in my family, thus I 'drifted' more and more into 'scientific thought', little by little, not knowing what was happening, but doing it nevertheless.

The scientific approach has become my worldview, and I am comfortable with it. Still, I am not so beholden by it, that I cannot allow for whatever may lie beyond it, its access prevented by a maintained paradigm, science. And here lies the explanation: Belief in the paradigm of science, no longer enables me to enter the spiritual paradigm I once experienced. Sure, I can still feel "as one with the world", but is is on an intellectual basis, as I expressed it in my verse "Belonging". So be it. I have used these latter three words quite frequently lately. They express my acceptance of whatever.

And yet, I must enter subsequently: I think it to be possible to enter such a state of mind at desire, if I really tried! It requires entering a trance, one can induce. Various spiritual people have done so, or at least claimed it. Kipling towards the end of his novel 'Kim' cites such an experience by his protagonist, and must therefore have experienced it, or be told of it, to be able to describe it so vividly.

The question that arises is, whether experiences of this nature are 'merely' an expression, a manifestation of the brain, its mind, even influenced by the respective belief system of the experiencer, or could it truly be real access to a universal spirit pervading the universe?

It is the 24th of December 2006. I just finished translating 200 poems of Karl May. I suppose I will continue my musings.

In the course, Ethics and Values, I'm presently taking, after a hiatus of two and one half years, I asked the facilitator to explain to the class of over 40 the meaning of the oft-used word 'philosophy', and he said 'love of knowledge'. I disagreed for the following reason. As the lecturer in the video series of this course points out, there is the difference between facts and values. Death is a fact, the big tsunami is, the sun burning hydrogen to helium is, but the interpretation of these facts is according to our values.

This is why I disagreed with the facilitator's definition! While knowledge is, or ought to be, at the base of our understanding of the world, being facts, it is the 'proper' interpretation of these facts by our values, which then result in 'wisdom'! Maybe! So, the primary meaning of 'sophy' is wisdom!

In other recent conversations I expressed that I am content where I am at this time of my life, content meaning, that I no longer strive for more further-out things. I have come to understand the limits of my mind and have accepted them. Subjects too esoteric, too far beyond my ability to understand, I can happily let be. Give me something more down to earth! In a brief exchange with a fellow course participant I said: When I recently held the door open for a woman with her small son, I was content. When, after she had said thank you, the little tike did so too, I was happy. Simple things like this have become more important. I also recall when I first came across the term 'pragmatism', when I still lived in Germany. Pragmatism was explained as a hallmark of American thought. It appealed to me, maybe it contributed to my coming to this country, and I think I followed its meaning.

Being content does not mean, however, that I've given up all attempts at 'understanding'. I still pursue. But, at my age of 70 now, I think I can be a bit more restrained.

Ute mentioned the other day, that she'd never be able to 'keep up with me', to fulfill my expectations. But then, she's just my associate 'sufferer' of what I did, maybe had to put upon me to compensate, to overcome that which put me back in my youth. And in one respect, I think, it did her good – both of us.

One more thing: Supposedly, the God of the Israelites said to them: I am, who I am.

Well, me, being nogod, say the same: I am, who I am!

Well – four years passed since my last writing, and I'm now headed towards 75 years of age. What's there to talk about? A number of things I wrote about have changed.

Only three months after joining, I dropped my board membership on the Yavapay Symphony Association since I couldn't stand the comittee work. I am used to making my own decisions – more or less. I took some courses at the Ollies, as the organisation calls itself nowadays, and dropped some that didn't appeal to me. I am no longer in contact with Marlies Bugmann, since her "know-it-all" attitude turned me off. I am finished with translating and the publication of 13 Karl May books. No more! Enough is enough! But I translated and self-published Sabine's book "One more Day . . ." on her behalf. And I had a hundred coppies of 99 of my poems printed and distributed more than half high and low. Maybe people, here and there, will make something of my writing. And, as a final task, I wrote the biography of Ute's grandparents and parents, which is now in the process of being printed and bound, but only for family members.

On July 8, 2011, Ute and I will celebrate our 50th wedding anniversary. For the 10th I/we will host 38 friends for dinner and libations at our favorite restaurant, the Tara Thai. The following day our family will "retreat" to Sedona for a few days.

Epilogue.

We did leave Germany, both at age 28, thus have lived now for 40 years in North America. Six of these years were spent in Canada, where we once thought vaguely in terms of becoming eventually Canadian citizens. Then came the company transfer to the USA and another vague thought arose: Where will we end up next? In the course of time any thought of becoming US citizens has receded further and further, if it ever really existed. Just last year now, we renewed our Green Cards, our permits as Resident Aliens to stay for another 10 years. When they expire we will be, with some luck, 78 years old. A few years ago I wrote for myself a little poem expressing my sentiment toward this issue. I called it:

Belonging:

I am – born German
at Home in America
yet at heart European
by Intellect Western Man
Human by Species
Member of all Life by Evolution
Part of the Universe by Chemistry.

And one day I shall return to it – not that I haven't been part of it all along – but in my physical constituents. I have asked my children, also Ute, thinking with both her parents having made it to 93 years of age, while the oldest in my family, my father, left at age 79, that I will go first (but who knows). In this case I ask to be cremated. Then, if possible, that they will carry me up to the top of Pine Mountain, where I have been. It's about 20 miles east of Interstate 17 in, what's left of the Wilds of Arizona. There, on a windy day, carefully staying upwind, empty the little, but amazingly heavy container, and commit me to the wind.

Ute's only complaint was, that I ought to go early before she's unable to make it the 11 miles to the top of Pine Mountain in this Wilderness Area. But from up there, one can almost see forever.

I might as well bring this entire story to a close by asking, that if and when someone will talk about me, that he or she stick to the truth. I wouldn't want to hear only 'good things', no I would want to hear all, the stark naked truth. Like in another context when I said: I'm German with all the warts. Should you be playing any music, make it J.S. Bach's Orchestral Suites 1-4, the last set, number 6, of Suite #2. Bach, a serious man, who composed, as he said: 'For the glory of God and the enjoyment of man', has written here a joyful, often lighthearted piece. And in Bach and Beethoven my people have added something very worthwhile to the heritage of man! Now, to be quiet, let me say:

Farewell

Now that my consciousness depart'd forever
I wish to tell you, here and now:
How much I loved you, Ute, Dearest,
but now it's time to say good bye.
In a hundred years I'll be forgotten,
and that is how it well should be,
so many others came before,
at best, I'll be a mark on the family tree.
If soul possessed me –
now gone for good –
will it linger for a while in thee?
In the hereabouts,
life's deeds committed,
they had their meaning
as they should...
I wish you well for years to come,
live happily and fill your life.
And when it comes to our failings:
So what! Did we not try the best we could?
I did my "things" through joy and strife,
with some regrets, as I surely should!
You stuck with me through "thick and thin",
and in the end – lo – did we win!
But, may I tell you now in closing:
Could I have had a better wife!
Love, Herbert